NUGGETS OF GOLD

NUGGETS OF GOLD

WISDOM FOR PRISONERS BY 12 EX-CONS

Power Publishing

PO Box 281

Lone Jack, MO 64070-0281

Nuggets of Gold

by 12 Ex-Cons

www.prisonpowerministries.org

Cover design and layout by Kevin Williamson

www.kevinwilliamsondesign.com

Edited by Debbie and Bill Corum

www.debbiecorum.com

ISBN 978-0-9895249-8-8

Printed in the United States of America

DEDICATION

This book is dedicated to all the men and women who are presently living or have lived behind walls, razor-wire fences, and gun towers. It's also to any who are out on paper or have walked that paper down.

ABOUT NUGGETS OF GOLD

Congratulations on picking up this little book. It may be small, but it is powerful. It's powerful, because it is full of words of encouragement and daily goals. Many of the words are from the Bible, which makes it immensely powerful.

It was written by former drug addicts, dealers, alcoholics, thieves, and every one of them have been where you are—sitting in a jail cell or locked up behind the walls, razor wire, and gun towers. Each contributor to this book has a desire to see men and women set free in the spirit and in the natural. We want you to know that God loves you and has an incredible plan for your life. Each of us loves you from the bottom of our heart and wants nothing more than to see you set free. You may never be free from the concrete and steel, but you can be free on the inside. That is our prayer for you—that as you read these pages you will whisper to Him that you are tired of running and you will surrender your life completely to Him.

Many of you have heard people quote the scripture in John 8:32, *You shall know the truth, and the truth shall set you free.* But they leave out the most important part—*If you continue in My Word, then you are truly disciples of Mine; and you will know the truth, and the truth will make you free.* Read John 8:31-32 again. Jesus said, *If you continue in My Word.* We must stay in the Word. This book is designed to help you do that.

Whether you're already a Christian or are interested in becoming one, this book will hopefully help you want to grow closer to the only One who can bring you real, true and everlasting peace. Pursue Him with all your heart, with all your mind, and with all your strength. Your life will never be the same.

God bless you and keep you and make His face to shine upon you.

In HIS grip,

Bill Corum

II Corinthians 5:17

GLOSSARY OF PRISON TERMS

BESTIE: Partner or best friend

BID: Time in prison

BOP: Bureau of Prisons

BUNK: Your bed

BUSTED: Arrested or caught

CELL: Your house, where you live

CELLIE: The person living in the same cell with you

CHOW TIME: When you go eat

CO: Corrections Officer

COMMISARY: The store in prison or jail

COUNTY: County jail

HOMEBOYS: People from your state or city, someone you run with

HOMIE: Someone you are close to or someone from your city or area

JAIL-HOUSE RELIGION: using religion as a tool to get out, or make early parole

MAINLINE: Out of reception and in general population

MONEY ON BOOKS: Having money available to use at commissary or store

ORANGE JUMPSUITS: Clothes worn by a certain class of inmate

RAZOR WIRE: The wire generally on top of a high fence, with razor edges

ROAD DOGS: Your running buddies

STORE: Commissary

YARD: The area of the prison where you can exercise

ZOOS ZOOS and WHAM WHAMS: Junk food, cookies, candy, etc.

TABLE OF CONTENTS

ONE THING

Psalm 27:4-5 NKJV

One thing I have desired of the Lord, That will I seek: That I may dwell in the house of the Lord All the days of my life, To behold the beauty of the Lord, And to inquire in His temple. For in the time of trouble He shall hide me in His pavilion; In the secret place of His tabernacle He shall hide me; He shall set me high upon a rock.

I have desired a lot of wrong things in my past. Women I wasn't married to, drugs, money, and other traps that ultimately took away my freedom and sent me to prison.

Since making Jesus Lord of my life, I get to wake up every morning and desire the most important thing in this life. That is, a right relationship with God.

It's the one thing I can count on when my life gets in a jam—that Jesus is the rock that I can stand on. I have been doing that now for almost thirty years.

TODAY'S GOAL:

When you get in trouble, are you fixing your mind on God to help you? Or are you relying on the ways you used in the past, to cope? Make sure today you take time to pray through your struggles instead of stressing on them. It works every time. This is the one thing you can count on today that won't let you down. *Ray Stribling*

CHOW TIME

Matthew 4:4 KJV

But He answered and said, it is written, Man shall not live by bread alone, but by every word that proceedeth out of the mouth of God.

What does Jesus mean here? He says we shall not live by just eating, but by every word that comes from the mouth of God. He was quoting from Deuteronomy 8:3 in the Old Testament.

Bottom line is that the Word of God, the B.I.B.L.E. (basic instructions before leaving earth) is just as important to us believers as actually eating food. We cannot live or grow without a consistent, steady diet of it. It is the good stuff. Like Saturdays in the federal joint. Those are hamburger days. Or going to store and walking away with a bag of zoo zoos and wham whams.

It is virtually impossible to grow in your faith and become a follower of Jesus Christ, and please the Father without meditating on the Word of God on a consistent basis. Hide it in your heart. As you read and meditate on the Word you will get closer to God. He wants to be your very best friend, and how close you get is determined by you.

The Bible will keep you from sin, or sin will keep you from the Bible.

TODAY'S GOAL:

Ask God through the power of the Holy Spirit to give you a hunger for His Word. Before you begin reading, ask the Holy Spirit to help you discern and understand it.

Bill Corum

UNASHAMED

Luke 9:26 NKJV

For whoever is ashamed of Me and My words, of him the Son of Man will be ashamed when He comes in His glory, and in His Father's, and of the holy angels.

Walking down the mainline corridor to the chapel, my homeboys recognized me and yelled my name. "Hey Phil, What's up homie?" I just got to the reception center on a parole violation. I had recently given my life to Christ. My old homeboys were obviously wondering why I was in the church line. The main chapel was on the mainline, and we were still in orange jumpsuits. With head held high, I walked the rest of the way, glad to be living as a Christian with a new outlook on life. I was not ashamed that I had chosen to be a Christian.

During that last stay in prison, I found new friends to spend my time with, and realized the importance of who I hung out with on a regular basis. I still talked to my old friends, but my newfound relationship with Christ caused me to reflect on who I should consider close friends. Fellow Christians, who at first didn't seem as cool or as *convict like*, actually had the same new outlook on life. What an awesome thing to see people in a whole new way.

TODAY'S GOAL:

So, who have you been hanging out with? The Bible says light has no fellowship with darkness. Are they helping you have a better life, or are they bringing you down?

Phil Fisher

HAVE A VISION

Matthew 24:45-50 NKJV

Who then is a faithful and wise servant, whom his master made ruler over his household, to give them food in due season? Blessed is that servant whom his master, when he comes, will find so doing. Assuredly, I say to you that he will make him ruler over all his goods. But if that evil servant says in his heart, 'My master is delaying his coming,' and begins to beat his fellow servants, and to eat and drink with the drunkards, the master of that servant will come on a day when he is not looking for him and at an hour that he is not aware of . . .

Jesus gives us two choices in how we could live our lives in what appears to be an end-of-the-age generation. He said it would take wisdom, but it could be done. He asks the question, 'Who will be diligent in the Word and gain understanding about how to lead others by giving them proper insight in the due season?'.

TODAY'S GOAL:

Are you up for the challenge of Gods leadership plan for your life? What ways are you using the talents He gave you? Stop and think about the ways you have been leading others.

Lisa Stribling

CALLED TO CALL

Romans 1:5-6 BSB

Through Him and on behalf of His name, we receive grace and apostleship to call all those among the gentiles to the obedience that comes from faith and you also are among those who are called to belong to Jesus Christ.

The Christian walk was not designed to be a lonely one, even though you're in a lonely place. There are others around you who are called by His name as well. And there are some who don't know His name. Your mission in life is to spread the Gospel of Jesus Christ and to make disciples. Don't treat Christianity as a treasure that others can steal from you. You must treat it as a never-ending treasure that you give away abundantly. If you have wisdom that is from God, it was given to you to share.

If you have revelation, it has also been given to you to share. Do not forsake your brothers and sisters and hide hope. Just like the words to the classic children's song, "This little light of mine, I'm gonna let it shine", so let your light shine. Be a towering inferno that draws people to Christ like a moth to a flame.

TODAY'S GOAL:

Start a prayer meeting. You can begin by doing it once a week and work up to once a day. Your comfort will be in drawing together. There are others in your facility who feel lonely and forsaken by God. It is your duty to show them that He is a God of love and mercy!

Richy Bickle

WHO, ME . . . RIGHTEOUS?

Romans 8:3-4 PARAPHRASED

For what the law could not do in that it was weak through the flesh, God did by sending His own Son. Jesus condemned sin in the flesh and fulfilled in us the righteous requirements of the law.

By God's grace, He did this for us, because of His great love for us. Because of this, we are now justified freely by His grace (Romans 3:24). One person said that "justified" really means "just as if we had never sinned." Justified by Jesus! What a deal!

When I was locked up in county forty-two years ago, I didn't believe anything was free. When the preacher said these very words to me, it was just too good to be true. So, for a time I just forgot it. But the preacher kept on coming back to the county jail, declaring that Jesus was real, and wanted to "justify" me. He told me once I confessed Jesus as Lord, and believed that God raised Him from the dead, I would be saved. What did I have to lose? It was free. So, I did it. Seconds later, I was saved. If I died right then, I would spend eternity in heaven. I knew in my heart I was forgiven.

TODAY'S GOAL:

If you are not saved, you are on the way to a sinner's hell. There is no parole, and you will be eternally separated from Jesus. Repent of your sins, ask God to forgive you and He will. Remember, we are talking about free stuff here.

Don Castleberry

SUN SETS OVER THE RAZOR WIRE

Psalm 103:12 KJV

As far as the east is from the west, so far hath he removed our transgressions from us.

Sitting in a jail or prison yard watching the sun set is not something most would consider enjoyable. The sun rays glimmer off the high fence and razor wire, sort of like light crystals projecting into the air. But as you sit there and pray to the God of the sunrises and sunsets—the God who shines Light into the darkness—you can take to heart that verse.

The Lord Jesus Christ is the Light of Life. *Then spake Jesus again unto them, saying, I am the light of the world: he that followeth me shall not walk in darkness, but shall have the light of life* (John 8:12). Today, as I watch those beautiful sunsets from my front porch in the hills of Tennessee, I fully appreciate that our God is a great God and full of forgiveness. Even as far as the east is from the west, His forgiveness is infinite and unmeasurable through Christ Jesus.

TODAY'S GOAL:

Thank God for that infinite and limitless forgiveness. Thank Him and praise Him, even through the high fence and razor wire. *Mickey Park*

SURRENDER

Isaiah 64:8 ESV

But now, O LORD, you are our Father; we are the clay, and you are our potter; we are all the work of your hand.

Before I was saved in prison, I wanted to change my life but was powerless to do so. I learned that I could not change me. If I could have changed me, I would have done so long before I was addicted, depressed, suicidal, homeless, lonely, lost, and eventually incarcerated! Is this also true of you? Have you tried to change yourself?

I tried to change myself an endless number of times but failed every time. So, it was great news to me that God did not expect me to change myself. Really. He only wanted me to allow His Holy Spirit to possess me, be willing daily to allow Him to lead me in the right way, and to try my best to instantly obey His promptings.

When we willingly surrender to God the Holy Spirit in us, and daily submit to be led by His Spirit instead of being led by our *flesh*, He will begin His work of sanctification in us. In other words, when we surrender to the Spirit, and submit to His leadership moment by moment, He will change us. We are not responsible for changing ourselves.

TODAY'S GOAL:

Ask the Holy Spirit to help you learn to surrender daily to His leadership. Decide today to submit to God in every way, every day. Let Him change you. Stop trying to change yourself.

Stephen Canup

REST, MY FRIEND

Matthew 11:28 ESV

Come to Me, all you who labor and are heavy laden, and I will give you rest.

Does this verse mean even after I've blown every concept of life that could be messed up—even the street life because I ended up in prison—I could come to Him? Could I really start a brand-new life? How? In 1991, in a prison bunk after thirty obnoxious, ignorant arrests, I read a tract that told me to confess my sins and realized I needed to make a serious attempt to find God. I had no concept of God or ever been to church. I asked God to give me a new life. I confessed my sins from ages ten- to twenty-four-years-old, which took three nights, crying out from my bunk. I didn't know you could confess all your sins at the same time. I gave up the wheel for God to drive this new life.

My God will come in and have your back for the rest of your life (Isaiah 41:10).

He is inviting you today, saying, "Come to Me". We need to be all in; just like running bars, streets, dope holes. All in to enter and remain in His rest.

I now finally have rest in my life. I know Jesus is always present with me, every second . . . in the good and bad. He is our friend during the difficulties most of us bring on ourselves.

TODAY'S GOAL:

Find a place to be alone with God. Speak to Him, seek Him, and find His rest.

Scott Heburn

THE SWITCH

Romans 4:24-25 NKJV

... but also for us. It shall be imputed to us who believe in Him who raised up Jesus our Lord from the dead, who was delivered up because of our offenses and was raised because of our justification.

I remember when the *switch* referred to a worldly street move. Some of those switches, the devil taught us and used against us. Thank God that His Word is so much greater and true. Jesus made the switch in our place when He went through what we should have gone through—death because of our sins!

Today's Scripture talks about the switch. *It shall be imputed to us who believe in Him*... Because of the switch, He who is now in us is greater than he who is in the world (John 4:4). Once we accept the switch by believing in Jesus wholeheartedly, we switch from dark to light, and become the children of God (1 Peter 2:9-10). *No longer be conformed to this world [any longer with its superficial values and customs] but be transformed* . . . Be switched to the kingdom of God. Why? The verse goes on to say, *So that you may prove [for yourselves] what the will of God is, that which is good and acceptable and perfect [in His plan and purpose for you]* (Romans 12:2).

This is all about God and you. He needs you to know why He stepped in on your behalf, (the switch). Salvation is God giving us a chance to start over again.

TODAY'S GOAL:

Ask God the Father, through the power of the Holy Spirit, to show you for yourself why you are so important to Him. Then ask the Holy Spirit to help you just believe and receive it!

Spencer Lindsay

THE NEED TO BE TRANSFORMED

Romans 12:2 AMP

And do not be conformed to this world [any longer with its superficial values and customs], but be transformed and progressively changed [as you mature spiritually] by the renewing of your mind [focusing on godly values and ethical attitudes], so that you may prove [for yourselves] what the will of God is, that which is good and acceptable and perfect [in His plan and purpose for you].

This Scripture commands you to be transformed in your mind, which is part of your soul. The word *transformed* (*metamorphoó*) means "the change of moral character for the better." Once you are born again, your spirit man has perfect morals. It never acts stupid. In fact, the Bible says you are the righteousness of God in Christ. But your soul, which includes your mind, needs to be renewed and changed so that it can walk in the righteousness that has been won for you.

Notice that Romans 12:2 says your soul transformation happens *progressively*. That means the healing of your mind and your inner man doesn't take place instantly when you get saved. Rather, as you will soon see, it unfolds step-by-step as you apply the power and presence of Jesus Christ.

TODAY'S GOAL:

Being transformed in your mind and the other parts of your soul will cause you to experience massive breakthrough. Turn Romans 12:2 into prayer. Tell God you do not want to be conformed to the world, but you want Him to renew your mind. Pray that Scripture daily for the next thirty days.

Katie Souza

SEEDTIME AND HARVEST

Genesis 8:22 NKJV

While the earth remains, Seedtime and harvest . . . day and night, shall not cease.

Did you know that seedtime and harvest are laws? Inside a cold cell the Holy Spirit spoke to me through this verse. Day and night, I was reaping a deserved harvest from the bad seeds I'd sown—drug trafficking, stealing jets, etc. "Twenty-two years," said the judge. Harvest time! *Do not be deceived, God is not mocked; for whatever a man sows, that he will also reap* (Galatians 6:7). Proverbs says that God was laughing at my calamity (Proverbs 1:26), *until* I repented. Then everything changed. I tossed out my bad seed bag and Jesus gave me a bag of good seeds. The new seeds I sowed were good, and the harvest became good. It took time for the bad harvest to die off, but eventually it did, and my prison time became easier. *So I say, walk by the Spirit, and you will not gratify the desires of the flesh* (Galatians 5:16). Eventually, I walked down those years, got out, continued to sow good, and never looked back. You can change your harvest by changing your seed. It's a spiritual law.

TODAY'S GOAL:

Choose Jesus. Take up the good seed bag and start sowing this Scripture-based proclamation: *But the fruit of the Spirit is love, joy, peace, patience, kindness, goodness, faithfulness, gentleness, self-control; against such things there is no law. Now those who belong to Christ Jesus have crucified the flesh with its passions and desires* (Galatians 5:22-24). *David Hairabedian*

OH, TASTE AND SEE

Psalm 34:8-9 NKJV

Oh, taste and see that the Lord is good; Blessed is the man who trusts in Him! Oh, fear the Lord, you His saints! There is no want to those who fear Him.

God is so good. Like your favorite zoo zoos and wham whams. If you are not walking with Him, then you don't have an opportunity to get a taste of Him. But if you are a believer and are truly seeking a close relationship with Him, then you will begin to see.

Our job as Christians is to live our lives in such a way that causes others to be inspired to find God. To make them hungry for what we have. Our choices are an expression of the Lord's goodness to us. There is truly nothing God won't do for those who trust in Him and believe. We will receive blessings just for trusting in Him.

TODAY'S GOAL:

Are you living your life in such a way that makes others want to find out what makes you full of peace? Does your joy from knowing God cause others to want to be around you and learn from you? Are you living in front of people the way you live in private? Decide today to inspire someone to live right by watching your life. *Ray Stribling*

FORGIVENESS

Matthew 6:13-15 KJV

And lead us not into temptation, but deliver us from evil: For thine is the kingdom, and the power, and the glory, forever. Amen. For if ye forgive men their trespasses, your heavenly Father will also forgive you: But if ye forgive not men their trespasses, neither will your Father forgive your trespasses.

Here is one of those passages that we struggle with. Jesus actually said, if we don't forgive those who have done something against us, God our Father will not forgive us. The daughter of one of my friends was raped; he was going to take care of it his way. He came out of an east coast mafia and still had friends there. He was reaching for the phone to call one of the hit men he knew to take care of it. The phone rang, and it was his daughter. She said, "Daddy, we have to forgive him." They *did* forgive him.

You have probably had situations in your life like I have, where you didn't want to forgive someone. Some of those situations were really bad, and I could figure out a bunch of reasons to not forgive that person/or persons.

Forgiveness is not an option for a Christian. It is not easy, but with God all things are possible.

TODAY'S GOAL:

Ask the Holy Spirit to reveal anyone you need to forgive. Forgiveness is a choice and not a feeling. Ask Him to help you make that choice.

Bill Corum

TEMPTATION

1 Corinthians 10:13 NKJV

No temptation has overtaken you except such as is common to man; but God is faithful, who will not allow you to be tempted beyond what you are able, but with the temptation will also make the way of escape, that you may be able to bear it.

I was thinking lately, how since becoming a Christian, I can now live like He (God) wants me to, because of His Word. When I first got out of prison, I was tempted like never before. However, when I quoted Scripture, or said it in my head, it seemed like the temptation would disappear. When I realized how much the Scriptures were helping me, I wrote down certain verses that helped me and stuck them in my wallet. When I started thinking about something I shouldn't—like lust or hate—I would pull those verses out and say them. Sometimes I said them to myself, and sometimes out loud. One of my favorites was and is, 1 Corinthians 10:13.

Now, even years later, those verses are as powerful as ever. Hebrews 4:12 tells us that the Word of God is *sharper than any two-edged sword.* God's Word is more powerful than any temptation that comes knocking on your door.

TODAY'S GOAL:

Ask God to show you when you are being tempted. Memorize or write down Bible verses that would help you with thoughts that try to tempt you. When the temptation comes, speak His Word. *Phil Fisher*

OH! MY MOUTH!

Psalm 39:1-4 NKJV

I said, "I will guard my ways, Lest I sin with my tongue; I will restrain my mouth with a muzzle, While the wicked are before me." I was mute with silence, I held my peace even from good; And my sorrow was stirred up. My heart was hot within me; while I was musing, the fire burned.

David talks about guarding his ways in Psalm 39. What He is actually talking about is guarding his mouth. He realized he had some very strong opinions that were driving his feelings. He knew if he spoke, he would later regret it. Oh, how our mouth can move without us even wanting it to. I think this is the best advice David ever gave anyone. If I can't figure out how to use my mouth properly, don't use it at all. Better said—keep it closed.

TODAY'S GOAL:

I want to encourage you in a three-day challenge to learn to control your speech. Go for three whole days without talking. Learn, like David, to put a muzzle on when its most needed instead of running into the same old problem over and over.

Lisa Stribling

YES, I'M TALKING TO YOU

Matthew 5:43-45 NKJV

You have heard that it was said, 'You shall love your neighbor and hate your enemy.' But I say to you, love your enemies, bless those who curse you, do good to those who hate you, and pray for those who spitefully use you and persecute you, that you may be sons of your Father in heaven;...

The first time I read this I thought, this is the most ridiculous and impossible thing that anybody could do. To be honest with you, it is. But we're not just anybody. We have the Spirit of God that lives in us. So, things that are impossible to mere mortals are within our reach. When the Word says to *bless your enemy*, that doesn't mean praying that God would change them into a better person like you, because frankly, you're not that cool either. It's about actually blessing their life. It's about being invested in the person who annoys you the most. Maybe it's your cellie, maybe it's a significant other, or a guard that never speaks kind words to you. It doesn't matter who it is or how badly they make you feel. This verse applies to your Christianity and there are no exceptions to it.

TODAY'S GOAL:

Here is your twenty-one-day challenge. Pray five times a day for the person you dislike the most. Pray for their family, pray that they would be blessed, even in their finances. If you do this, I promise you will feel differently about this person at the end of twenty-one days. I know because it's the way I live my life. Something miraculous happens when we pray for those we hate.

Richy Bickle

THE FEAR OF THE LORD

Psalms 19:9 NKJV

The fear of the LORD is clean, enduring forever . . .

Proverbs 1:7 NKJV

The fear of the LORD is the beginning of knowledge . . .

What does the fear of the Lord mean? It is to have an awe or reverence for God as Creator, Mighty God, All Powerful, and fully recognizing Him as who He really is—God Almighty!

How do we find out who God really is? God gave us His Word. It's called the Holy Bible. We need to read and study it. When was the last time you read it?

Someday, we will all stand before a Holy God and Jesus and give account for our lives. All that we have ever done or said is recorded. Now is the time to search your heart. Do you really have the fear of God in your heart, and do you love Him?

Remember that first time you got dressed down by a guard? You were a brand-new inmate, in new prison clothes, didn't even know where the chow hall was located. You learned respect after that. So fear God. Respect Him. *The Lord of hosts, Him you shall hallow, let Him be your fear, and let Him be your dread* (Isaiah 8:13).

TODAY'S GOAL:

Read your Bible every day. Start with the book of John. Read it four times to start. Read it out loud if you can. Why out loud? Because faith comes by hearing the Word of God.

Don Castleberry

HE LOVED US, EVEN IN OUR SINS

Romans 5:8 KJV

But God commendeth his love toward us, in that, while we were yet sinners, Christ died for us. Much more then, being now justified by his blood, we shall be saved from wrath through him.

Recently, while preaching to a group of inmates in a drug recovery program in a prison, I was playing a music video about the love and mercy of God. The Holy Spirit spoke to my heart and said that Christ loved us even in our sinful state. That touched my heart deeply. I shared with the men that it is not just when you start going to church, or Bible study, or reading your Bible, but Christ loved us when we were wallowing in sin and in the gutters of addiction. In the Bible, He loved the prostitute, the leper, the shackled demon possessed, all while they were still sinners. *That while we were yet sinners*... That to me, is overwhelming, mind-boggling love.

TODAY'S GOAL:

God's love is not something you earn or work for. It is not a paycheck or something you get through your own efforts. God's love is for you today, right where you are. No strings attached. You can be justified and fully receive that love as you trust Jesus Christ today. *Mickey Park*

RESCUE ME

Psalm 69:14-15 NIV

Rescue me from the mire, do not let me sink; deliver me from those who hate me, from the deep waters. Do not let the floodwaters engulf me or the depths swallow me up or the pit close its mouth over me.

Psalm 40:1-2 NIV

I waited patiently for the Lord; He turned to me and heard my cry. He lifted me out of the slimy pit, out of the mud and mire . . .

God has plenty of experience pulling people up out of their own miry, dark, damp, deep pits. David, a man after God's own heart, must have known exactly what it was like because he wrote these Psalms above.

Before I went to prison, I lived for years in hopelessness and despair. Having been previously diagnosed as bi-polar, I lived in an almost constant state of suicidal depression. Homeless and helpless, I thought nothing would ever get better in any way. Frozen in fear of what might happen if I ever tried to climb out, I sunk lower and lower into what I was sure was a bottomless black-hole pit.

When I finally admitted I could not help myself and turned to Him in true humility, God was ready, willing, and able to step in, reach down, and pull me out.

Can you see yourself sinking? Are you bogged down? Are you finally ready to stop trying to save yourself? Cry out for help.

TODAY'S GOAL:

Reach out to God. Call on the name of Jesus. He will give you peace. He will rescue you. Let Him.

Stephen Canup

THANK YOU, JESUS

Ephesians 2:8-9 NKJV

For by grace you have been saved through faith, and that not of yourselves; it is the gift of God, not of works, lest anyone should boast.

When I'd done nothing right in my life, I found a Savior with arms open wide, ready to give me a second chance at life. Drugs, alcohol, and crime brought death to some of my friends who didn't get that second chance. If you have breath, you have a second chance.

It's hard to believe grace is a free gift. We still do certain things, thinking it will make God mad or glad at us. God's love toward us is unconditional. He wants what's best for us. We need to quit beating ourselves up over sin and thank Jesus for forgiving us. Realizing what He did, gives us the power to overcome sin and live in freedom and peace.

Jesus took care of the world's sin problem by suffering on the cross. We are to put our faith in Him, not in ourselves. We are to love, trust, and obey Him the best we can. He takes care of the rest. God's plan for your life is magnificent. Keep your faith in Him, not in yourself. Jesus is the only one who can forgive sins.

It's all by God's grace and forgiveness through faith. Thank you, Jesus, for making it easy on us knuckleheads.

TODAY'S GOAL:

Take this chance at a new life. Be all in for God just like you were all in for the devil. Fall endlessly, hopelessly, deeply in love with the God who adores you and is on your side.

Scott Heburn

TWO CHOICES

Deuteronomy 30:19 NKJV

I call heaven and earth as witnesses today against you, that I have set before you life and death, blessing and cursing; therefore choose life, that both you and your descendants may live;

I never ever imagined that in life there are only two choices and out of those two choices the consequences are either life or death, blessings or curses. Notice in today's Scripture that those choices also affect our descendants, (in other words our children).

While I was in prison, my life changed for the better after I read this Scripture and took it to heart.

We must weigh our choices everyday by the Word of God. And as we abide in the Word, our choices will start to look and sound like the Word (John 15:5).

Make every day you live, a day that you *choose* God's life over the devil's death. Your kids are counting on you!

TODAY'S GOAL:

Ask God, through the power of the Holy Spirit, to help you discern the consequences of every decision you make today. *Spencer Lindsay*

MADE UP OF THREE PARTS

I Thessalonians 5:23 NKJV

Now may the God of peace Himself sanctify you completely; and may your whole spirit, soul, and body be preserved blameless at the coming of our Lord Jesus Christ.

God created you as a three-part being. All you see is your body, but you also have a spirit and a soul in that body.

God's will is to sanctify every part of your body, soul, and spirit. When you received Jesus Christ into your life, your spirit was made instantly complete. The Bible says the same Spirit that lives in Christ now lives in you (Colossians 1:27). Because Christ is perfect, your spirit man is also flawless. It never sins, never gets upset, and always trusts God. Your spirit is now brand new. *Therefore, if anyone is in Christ, he is a new creation; old things have passed away; behold, all things have become new* (2 Corinthians 5:17).

You might think, If I am a totally new creation, how come I feel like a wreck and am acting worse? The answer is because when a person is born again, only one part of him is perfected. His body and soul—which is his mind, will, and emotions—still need healing.

TODAY'S GOAL:

God's will for us is to be whole in every part and He has provided the power to make this happen. Ask the Lord to fill you with His power to sanctify you completely.

Katie Souza

BAD CARDS

Psalm 51:5 KJV

Behold, I was shapen in iniquity; and in sin did my mother conceive me.

The first time I read this passage I was sitting in a prison cell and realized that we all start with a bad hand of cards at life's poker table. Every one of us, at birth, is full of iniquity and sin. Bad hand. Losing cards. Some just accept their fate and give up, or they might begin to look for the Royal Flush another way. Maybe you looked for it but in the wrong location: drug business, bank robbery, or by cheating. We were born knowing how to lie, cheat, and steal. 'Sin and iniquity' was our basic nature, just like the Bible says. It's not your fault. At birth you got Adam's nature, bad cards. Lousy DNA.

God offers a solution—a new nature, winning cards, a new DNA—available from a different dealer, Jesus Christ. You can call it the DNA-Divine Nature of the Almighty. You are His son, and you get to be just like your new Father. *If any man be in Christ he is a new creature, old things are passed away, all things are become new* (2 Corinthians 5:17-18).

TODAY'S GOAL:

Ask him for this new DNA nature to be infused into you now. Here is His promise to you today:

God made him who had no sin to be sin for us, so that in him we might become the righteousness of God (2 Corinthians 5:21).

David Hairabedian

DON'T FREAK OUT

Psalm 37:7-8 NKJV

Rest in the Lord and wait patiently for Him; Do not fret because of him who prospers in his way, Because of the man who brings wicked schemes to pass. Cease from anger and forsake wrath; Do not fret-It only causes harm.

One of the hardest things I had to do was overcome my impatience and not always freak out and get angry over situations that seemed to never turn out on my behalf. It was hard when I couldn't make things happen illegally after I became a Christian, the way it seemed everyone else was doing.

Eventually, I learned to trust God for different outcomes because I prayed. I hadn't learned to hide Bible verses in my heart yet like, *Trust in the Lord, don't lean on your own understanding, and He will direct your paths* (Proverbs 3:5-6).

Are you learning to rest in the truth that God loves you, and will fight for you to have the things you need?

TODAY'S GOAL:

Today, choose not to freak out in those stressful situations that are in front of you. Remember it only makes it worse. Exercise your faith and trust God for your needs!

Ray Stribling

ADULTERY

Matthew 5:27-28 KJV

Ye have heard that it was said by them of old time, Thou shalt not commit adultery: But I say unto you, That whosoever looketh on a woman to lust after her hath committed adultery with her already in his heart.

I know what you're thinking. Come on, Bill, be reasonable. If you're reading this from the BOP or some state prison, county jail, or the streets, there is temptation there. A friend of mine wrote a book called *Covenant With My Eyes.* It is so heavy, I only give it to people who are extremely serious about following Jesus. This book will mess you up. I can't hardly watch the news on TV anymore because the weather lady has a dress on that is cut too low.

Have you ever been in a train wreck because your passions got misdirected? I certainly have—many times—and boy do I regret it.

Ed Cole wrote a book called *Maximized Manhood.* I was in a meeting once where he was the speaker. He said that sometimes temptation can overwhelm us and be tormenting. But here is a statement he made that you need to get in your heart. "The torment of the temptation to sin does not compare with the torment of the consequence of sin."

TODAY'S GOAL:

Ask Jesus by the power of the Holy Spirit to give you the power to walk in purity. Even while you are single.

Bill Corum

BROKEN RELATIONSHIPS

Psalm 127:4-5 NKJV

Like arrows in the hand of a warrior, So are the children of one's youth. Happy is the man who has his quiver full of them . . .

Children are a gift from God. The Bible says that they are like arrows in a quiver.

My children never knew me because I stayed locked up for most of their lives. I used to write to them once in a while to see if I could get a response, and none would come. Then one day, I read a Christian newspaper. In it, there was an article where an inmate said he had the same problem. The inmate in the article came up with an ingenious idea. Instead of writing a regular letter, he wrote out puzzles, such as word searches to find the hidden word. Sure enough, just a few days after sending off my first puzzle to my kids, I got my first return letter. Many more followed.

I'd like to tell you that everything was great from then on, but the truth is, it was a healing process that took time. God helped me along the way. Now, twenty-five-years later, my daughter and granddaughter are a part of my life. I am thankful to God for restoring broken relationships.

TODAY'S GOAL:

Ask God to restore the broken relationships in your life. Forgive those who have hurt you and ask God to help those you may have hurt. Give it time and trust Him to help you.

Phil Fisher

LOVE SEES ME

Psalm 18:16-19 NKJV

He sent from above, He took me; He drew me out of many waters. He delivered me from my strong enemy, From those who hated me, For they were too strong for me. They confronted me in the day of my calamity, But the Lord was my support. He also brought me out into a broad place; He delivered me because He delighted in me.

Do you ever feel like no one sees you—like love can't find you? Maybe you feel like you don't have a name that anyone knows. That this season in your life may go on forever. Well, that is a lie! Heaven knows your name. In fact, God has it written on the palm of His hand, and the very hairs of your head are all numbered. Just think about it— God found you because He delights in you.

TODAY'S GOAL:

Read all of Psalm 18 and start praying it over yourself. You will begin to see God does not deliver you from your struggles because He has to, or because you earn His help. He delivers you because He likes us. Try that on for a day.

Lisa Stribling

IF IT WERE EASY, EVERYONE WOULD DO IT

Matthew 7:13,14 NKJV

Enter by the narrow gate; for wide is the gate and broad is the way that leads to destruction, and there are many who go in by it. Because narrow is the gate and difficult is the way which leads to life, and there are few who find it.

The biggest lie in Christianity, is that now life will be easy. Nowhere in the Bible does it say that. In fact, it says the opposite. Only through persecution, trials, and pressures do we become who God wants us to be. Think about this—every disciple was executed except for John. Jesus' whole car got wiped out, his clique was decimated, and He saw it as good because God has a heavenly perspective and knows what eternity means. Prepare your heart for struggle, especially in an environment like prison. You have the tools to overcome all battles that come your way. You just have to answer the bell every time, to win the fight. That's all it takes. Narrow is the path but glorious is the end.

TODAY'S GOAL:

Do something to make yourself uncomfortable. Whether it be talking to someone who the rest of the prison deems unsuitable or saying a kind word to a guard because he is human too. Make your words count! Be a real Christian today. Bless those who curse you. Speak life when others speak death. If it were easy, everyone would do it. *Richy Bickle*

POWER OF THE HOLY SPIRIT

John 14:16-17 NKJV

I will pray the Father, and He will give you another Helper, that He may abide with you forever—the Spirit of truth, whom the world cannot receive . . .

The disciples of Jesus were sad, all twelve of them. Jesus had previously told them that He was leaving and that where He was going, they could not come. So Jesus encouraged them by telling them that the Helper—Holy Spirit—was going to come from God and would help them.

That sounded like so much fiction to them. Kind of like a prison official telling you that you are going home tomorrow after starting a twenty-year sentence. Uh oh. The preachers crucified Jesus on a cross, using the Roman soldiers. Jesus is dead. Where is the Helper now?

Jesus had told His disciples to stay in Jerusalem until they received power from on high. So they did; they obeyed. Then ten days later, it happened. Pentecost came (Acts 2). They were in an upper room, all 120 of them. Boom! Things got loud. All the people were baptized in Holy Spirit. They now had the power. They praised God.

TODAY'S GOAL:

Ask yourself: Are you born again? (Romans 10:9-10) Do you have the power? (Acts 2)

Don Castleberry

FROM ROCK BOTTOM

Psalm 40:1-3 KJV

I waited patiently for the Lord; and he inclined unto me, and heard my cry. He brought me up also out of an horrible pit, out of the miry clay, and set my feet upon a rock, and established my goings. And he hath put a new song in my mouth, even praise unto our God: many shall see it, and fear, and shall trust in the Lord.

Sometimes you just never really imagine how messed up and busted up your life will end up. Satan and sin will drag you down a long, hard road and leave you in a hemp pile of emptiness and devastation. My life, like many of yours, had hit *rock bottom* (99 year sentence). That is just the hard and harsh reality of sin and the consequences of those bad choices. It was at my rock bottom in life that I turned to the Lord Jesus Christ and He heard my cry. He will hear yours. You can go from rock bottom to the Rock of Calvary in Christ Jesus.

TODAY'S GOAL:

Let Christ Jesus reach into your rock bottom and take over your life. Let Him pour out His Love, Mercy, and Grace and pull you out of that horrible pit of your past.

Mickey Park

JAIL-HOUSE RELIGION

Luke 19:10 NKJV

...for the Son of Man has come to seek and to save that which was lost.

The religious leaders of the day wanted to know why Jesus ate with and ministered to "sinners". Where are there plenty of lost sinners? They are locked up in prison. Jesus is seeking to save us.

In prison, we are sober and in our right minds. And we are still. If we listen, we can hear Him here. Isn't this the time and place that makes the most sense to cry out to God?

Can someone really find God in a jail or prison? Is God close enough to us to hear our sincere cry? Can we really be heard by Him as we commit, or re-dedicate our hearts to walk with Christ? Can He actually use a convict who turns his life around, to advance the cause of His Kingdom? *Jail-house religion*, a term we have all heard in a negative light, does not have to be a cheap imitation. Rather, it can be *the real thing*. God can change you forever, but you must let Him. You must want to be changed. It begins with absolute surrender and submission to His will for you.

TODAY'S GOAL:

Are you ready to surrender to God? Tell our Heavenly Father you are ready to submit your life and your will to His plan. Trust Him one day at a time to lead you by His Holy Spirit, into His future for you. Begin today.

Stephen Canup

STORMS AND TROUBLING TIMES

1 Corinthians 10:13 NKJV

No temptation has overtaken you except such as is common to man; but God is faithful, who will not allow you to be tempted beyond what you are able, but with the temptation will also make the way of escape, that you may be able to bear it.

When we do bad, we bring hurt and anguish upon ourselves and loved ones. Yet, other people who seem good can also have bad things happen. All of us have storms in our lives. Let's quit looking at the storm and look for Jesus in the storm. Jesus is *always* in the storm with us. He's the way of escape.

We are in troubling, painful times. Know that God will pursue and take care of us sufficiently. Use what God shows you through this experience, to reach others. We need to be a light to those around us, showing them that there is victory. When I went to prison, I couldn't see good coming out of it. Now, twenty-seven-years later, I'm sharing His love with you. Be Jesus to people, no matter the circumstance.

I, the Lord, have called You in righteousness, And will hold Your hand; I will keep You and give You as a covenant to the people, As a light to the Gentiles, to open blind eyes, to bring out prisoners from the prison . . . (Isaiah 42:6-7).

TODAY'S GOAL:

Meditate on the good Jesus is going to pull from this storm to benefit you, those who are incarcerated, and your loved ones. God is faithful.

Scott Heburn

STUCK PART 1

Romans 7:15 AMPC

For I do not understand my own actions [I am baffled, bewildered]. I do not practice or accomplish what I wish, but I do the very thing that I loathe [which my moral instinct condemns].

I was stuck right here in this Scripture for years and I did not know it. I got saved in a jail in 1992, but for the next eighteen years I was stuck. Saved, but stuck. Then I found out it was not me doing it, *but the sin [principle] which is at home in me and has possession of me* (Romans 7:17).

When I was in the streets, I always felt like something had me possessed because I would do some real crazy and stupid things. And I found myself under the influence of drugs every time, but I didn't realize the problem started in me (Romans 7-18-20).

As the Holy Spirit was leading me, He brought me to this—*and in a humble (gentle, modest) spirit receive and welcome the Word which implanted and rooted [in your hearts] contains the power to save your souls* (James 1:21). Save my soul? Yes, that is what it says. We have a soul problem, and if it is not fixed, we live in a stuck position in life. We find ourselves re-penting and repenting and repenting . . . and never getting free, which is called *stuck*!

TODAY'S GOAL:

Ask the Father by His Spirit to lead you out from this place called stuck. Allow the Holy Spirit to teach you about your soul. *Spencer Lindsay*

STUCK PART 2

John 14:30 NKJV

I will no longer talk much with you, for the ruler of this world is coming, and he has nothing in Me.

Why do you think Satan, the ruler of this world in 2 Corinthians 4:4—who Jesus is talking about in the above Scripture—has nothing in Jesus? Because Jesus never committed a sin. As for us, it is a whole different story. We have committed sins and even practice committing sins, and the Bible says when we sin, we wound our souls (Isaiah 30:26; Romans 7:20). But what do I do about the wounds in my soul caused by sin? Notice in Leviticus 17:11, that the blood atones for the soul.

If you have accepted Jesus as your Lord and Savior, you have a legal right to claim healing through His shed blood (Isaiah 53:4-6). Whenever you are seeking healing for your soul, the blood of Christ is the first and most effective medicine you can apply (Hebrews 9:22; 1 John 1:7).

But we cannot stop there. It is the cross, plus the empty tomb that tells the total story of our faith—the death and the resurrection. The power of the resurrection radiates out from the empty tomb, giving all believers the ability to live in victory. But most of us are not aware because I was not aware (Philippians 3:10). Read *Healing the Wounded Soul* by Katie Souza.

TODAY'S GOAL:

Ask the Holy Spirit to led you to the things that the enemy has in common with you. Then start pleading the blood of Jesus over what He shows you!

Spencer Lindsay

TRAUMA WOUNDS THE SOUL

Job 10:1 AMP

I am disgusted with my life and loathe it! I will give free expression to my complaint; I will speak in the bitterness of my soul.

This world is a traumatic place to live. Every day I hear horror stories from people around the globe describing devastating situations in their relationships, finances, or other areas. These can bring trauma. Read about Job, whose story is described in the book of Job. He experienced horrible traumas (Job 1:13-19; 2:7).

Unrepented iniquities of our ancestors can also cause trauma. Prisons and jails can add even more to our already traumatized lives. And the worst thing about trauma is—it's deadly. It can wound your soul, drive you to sin, cause sickness, and destroy the rest of your life. The apostle Paul said in Romans 7:20, *Now if I do what I do not desire to do, it is no longer I doing it [it is not myself that acts], but the sin [principle] which dwells within me [fixed and operating in my soul].*

TODAY'S GOAL:

Ask God to show you where trauma in your life has caused wounds to your soul. Ask Him to begin healing you today. *Lord Jesus, I ask that You heal all the wounds in my soul. I believe that You can wash me clean of any sin that wounded me, heal me of every trauma I have lived through, and wipe out all generational iniquities and wounds in my bloodline. I believe that You are the lover of my soul and will give me breakthrough in every area I need healing. I praise You and thank You in advance for the victory! In Jesus' Name, amen.*

Katie Souza

BUY FOOD WITH NO MONEY

Isaiah 55:1-2 NKJV

Ho! Everyone who thirsts, Come to the waters; And you who have no money Come, buy and eat. Yes, come, buy wine and milk Without money and without price. Why do you spend money for what is not bread, And your wages for what does not satisfy? Listen carefully to Me, and eat what is good, And let your soul delight itself in abundance.

That word, *Ho*, was designed to get your attention. The word *Everyone* is just what it says—all. No one is excluded. That means you and me. How cool is that? Can you imagine being able to go to the commissary with no limit, and no money on your books? And get anything you wanted? Let alone buy wine there. But every single day God offers the wine of His refreshing Spirit to us freely without paying a dime for it. And His Spirit is sure to satisfy us without leaving us with a hangover!

TODAY'S GOAL:

What do you spend energy on that is never going to satisfy you? Make a list, give them to God, and then throw that list in the trash. Start today off fresh by praying and seeking God to satisfy you. Sing a song of thanksgiving to Jesus for all that He has done for you. *Ray Stribling*

RESTORATION

Malachi 4:6 KJV

And he shall turn the heart of the fathers to the children, and the heart of the children to their fathers, lest I come and smite the earth with a curse.

This verse means so much to me because I prayed it and spoke it back to God for almost five years. The Bible says to remind God of His Word (Isaiah 62:6). He knows what it says, He just likes for us to speak or pray it back to Him.

If you've read my life story *The Ultimate Pardon*, you know that I had no relationship with my four children because of choices I made. God completely repaired that mess. He will do the same for you. If you begin by humbling yourself (James 4:6), He will give you grace to stand.

I don't think we have a drug problem, crime problem, prison overcrowding problem. We have a father problem.

I always ask men in prison how many of them have children. Almost all of them raise their hands. Then I ask how many aren't in touch with their children. An overwhelming amount raise their hands. We definitely have a father problem!

TODAY'S GOAL:

Start by asking the Holy Spirit to help you understand how much God wants your family fixed. He is in the business of mending broken lives, relationships with family, and marriages. Ask God to give you a strategy to reach out to your children. It didn't get broke overnight and it won't get fixed overnight. Do not rush it! *Bill Corum*

COMING TO CHRIST

Romans 8:38-39 NKJV

For I am persuaded that neither death nor life, nor angels nor principalities nor powers, nor things present nor things to come. nor height nor depth, nor any other created thing, shall be able to separate us from the love of God which is in Christ Jesus our Lord.

My coming to Christ was not out of fear for what kind of hell awaited me. Neither was it through fear of death. I had already come close to death through overdoses on three separate occasions. It is a miracle that I am alive today.

I came to Christ because I realized how much He really loved me. Even after all the terrible things I did. Knowing every thought and every deed, He still loved me. That was hard to fathom.

You may think that you are beyond God's love because of how you have lived your life. Exactly the opposite is true. The Bible tells us in Romans 5:8, *But God demonstrates His own love toward us, in that while we were still sinners, Christ died for us.* He loved us even while we were still sinning, and chose to die for us, so that we could live with Him.

TODAY'S GOAL:

God loves you. Come to Him believing that nothing will ever be able to separate you from His love. When doubts and fears arise in your heart, speak His words of love over yourself.

Phil Fisher

THANK YOU FOR THE CROSS

Psalm 22:16-18 NKJV

For dogs have surrounded Me; The congregation of the wicked has enclosed Me. They pierced My hands and My feet; I can count all My bones. They look and stare at Me. They divide My garments among them, And for My clothing they cast lots.

There was a moment in time when Jesus was in this scenario, hanging on the cross. I can imagine the Father looking at Him and then having to turn away. Choosing to let Him go through the awful pain so that you and I could be reconciled with the Father and get into heaven. Oh, how very painful this must have been. Luke 22:19-20 tells us, This is my body which is given for you . . . and this is my blood that has been poured out for you.

TODAY'S GOAL:

Take communion daily and remember what Jesus did for you that day on the cross. Find elements that represent His body and His blood that was shed for you. Jesus said all our sins would be covered and all our diseases would be healed. Why not claim this daily over your life by eating the communion? Oh, I'm so thankful for the cross!

Lisa Stribling

TAKE YOUR THOUGHTS CAPTIVE!

Philippians 4:8 NKJV

Finally, brethren, whatever things are true, whatever things are noble, whatever things are just, whatever things are pure, whatever things are lovely, whatever things are of good report, if there is any virtue and if there is anything praiseworthy—meditate on these things.

I remember like it was yesterday, spending time in my cell daydreaming about things that were never going to happen. Fantasizing about crimes I would commit and revenge I would plot. Nothing good was in me because my thoughts were filled with wickedness. I didn't think of the mercy of God in my life, that He would take a sixteen-year old in a maximum-security prison and keep him safe. I thought it was my own cunning and wicked brain which was always set on evil. What could I have been if I had used that time, instead, to meditate on the blessings in my life while I was in prison? They were abundant, but I just didn't see them.

The whole struggle of this Christian walk will be fought inside your head. So, why not focus on the positive? Stay away from the drama instead of being a part of the drama and propagating nothing but negativity.

TODAY'S GOAL:

Focus on the positives in your life. For one, you're not going to burn in hell and that's pretty positive. So, if you can't find anything else, start there and God will begin to meet you and answer your weak *yes*!

Richy Bickle

TOTAL SURRENDER PART I

Romans 13:1 AMPC

Let every person be loyally subject to the governing (civil) authorities. For there is no authority except from God [by His permission, His sanction], and those that exist do so by God's appointment.

First, let's get it straight about what authorities you need to be submissive to. According to this Scripture—all of them! The Bible makes it clear; there is not one cop or judge who hasn't been placed in their position except by God, so you need to submit to them all. What happens when you don't?

. . . He who resists and sets himself up against the authorities resists what God has appointed and arranged [in divine order]. And those who resist will bring down judgment upon themselves [receiving the penalty due them] (Romans 13:2).

My co-defendants and I fought our case for almost two years. During this time, we were transported to a federal courthouse for numerous hearings. On those trips, I would wreak total havoc with the federal marshals. As a result, they would throw me in the hole when I got back from court. Resisting authority was my normal behavior.

So what is my point in telling you all this?

Romans 13:2 says we bring judgement on ourselves when we resist authority. Have you ever considered that? I sure hadn't.

TODAY'S GOAL:

Ask God to help you see all authority as appointed by Him. Ask Him to help you to submit to them.

Katie Souza

TOTAL SURRENDER PART 2

Romans 13:2 AMPC

. . . He who resists and sets himself up against the authorities resists what God has appointed and arranged [in divine order]. And those who resist will bring down judgment upon themselves [receiving the penalty due them].

I know from first-hand experience that this Scripture is true. When you resist the authorities, you are directly resisting God and will face the consequences. God's plan of submission is designed to bless you. This may be hard to believe, especially when you need to submit to an official who seems totally unjust. However, the Bible promises if you obey that person God will bring *good* to you through them . . . *For he is God's servant for your good* (Romans 13:1, 4).

The judicial system is appointed by God for chastisement. Chastise means to discipline. One of the main functions of the judicial system is to restrain evil through punishment. When the law is enforced, fear of punishment will stop lawless behavior to some degree.

So, how can the C.O. who hassles you or the judge who gave you so much time possibly be a servant for your good? Let me tell you, my thirteen-year sentence prompted me to seek God in an intense way. I finally got so tired of being punished by the authorities that I stopped acting up and started seeking God with all my heart.

TODAY'S GOAL:

Tell God that you want to totally surrender to Him, and you need His help to submit to *all* authority.

Katie Souza

DO YOU REALLY WANT TO GET WELL?

John 5:6 NIV

When Jesus saw him lying there and learned that he had been in this condition for a long time, he asked him, "Do you want to get well?"

I read this passage the first time in 1990 while sitting in a prison cell and thought, this is the dumbest question Jesus ever asked anyone. The crippled guy is at the miracle pool of Bethesda. No one is there to help him to the pool when the angel stirs the water.

Then the Holy Spirit illuminated the real reason Jesus asked, *'Do you want to get well?'*. He reminded me of the many who attend church, go to gatherings, even ask for prayer at religious services, but few get healed. Suddenly, I saw Jesus' question as the smartest question ever. "Do you really want to get well?" I realized Jesus was asking me, and every prisoner, the same question. Do you want to get well? Or are you content in your situation as a cripple? Crippled by drug addiction, depression, anger, gang violence, pornography, alcohol, foul language—your crutches. The 2,000-year-old question from Jesus remains. "Do you want to get well?" If yes, then Jesus will heal you.

TODAY'S GOAL:

Ask Him now. From someone Jesus delivered in a prison cell, I promise He will set you free too! Jesus is *no respecter of persons* (Acts 10:34).

Scripture-based proclamation for strength: "I am dead to sin but alive to God in Christ Jesus my Lord" (Romans 6:11). *David Hairabedian*

THE MERCY OF GOD

Psalm 52:8 NKJV

But I am like a green olive tree in the house of God;
I trust in the mercy of the Lord forever.

As I entered that trustee tank, all the inmates looked at me. I was the new guy. No 'how are you?', or anything. One guy asked me, 'Did you bring any tobacco? You better have brought a can of tobacco.'.

I needed mercy from these tough-looking guys. As time went on, I learned the ropes so to speak.

Years later, God showed me that indeed, He had given me mercy that day, and I didn't learn about one mercy of God but several mercies that God gives us. God gives us undeserved mercy, as indeed all true mercy must be. For deserved mercy is only a misnomer for justice.

God gives us rich mercy. Some things are great, but don't last long. This mercy is healing to your drooping spirits and a golden ointment to your bleeding wounds.

God gives us manifold mercy. All the flowers in God's garden are double. God gives us abounding mercy. Millions have received it, yet it is far from being exhausted. It is always fresh, full, and free.

TODAY'S GOAL:

Call upon God. "Please have mercy on me. I am a sinner. I don't want justice. I want your mercy." When you repent, and confess your sins to God, you are forgiven.

Don Castleberry

GOD'S THOUGHTS—HIGHER THAN OURS

Isaiah 55:8-9 KJV

For my thoughts are not your thoughts, neither are your ways my ways, saith the Lord. For as the heavens are higher than the earth, so are my ways higher than your ways, and my thoughts than your thoughts.

The major battle of the mind and heart in all of us is our thought life. We must come to the real source of hope and help in our time of need—and that is God. In Christ Jesus we can find the peace and comfort that nothing else in this world gives. I know that sometimes things happen, that life is full of hurts, full of pain, death, sickness, and horrific tragedies. The courts and judges will deny you and disappoint you, family and friends will forsake you and leave you wondering why. Why Lord? This truth from the depths of Biblical knowledge and wisdom rings true: His ways are higher than our ways and His thoughts higher than our thoughts.

TODAY'S GOAL:

Trust God in and through it all. No matter the circumstances or how hard it seems, His ways are higher than ours. His thoughts are higher than ours. Realize that we may not know what tomorrow holds, but we know who holds tomorrow.

Mickey Park

STOP LISTENING TO OTHERS

Mark 5:40 NKJV

And they ridiculed Him (Jesus)...

Luke 23:11

Then Herod, with his men of war, treated Him with contempt and mocked Him...

Many inmates taunt Christians with stuff like, "You weren't reading your Bible on the street" or "You weren't going to church or chapel services before they locked you up" or "Man, that's just that old jail-house religion, it will wear off pretty soon. It's not real. It's just the same old fake stuff we've seen before." I heard all that too.

In one respect, they were right. I don't know about you, but if I had been caught up in God's Word instead of my addictions, I wouldn't have ended up in prison. If I had been going to church every week instead of going out to beg, borrow, or steal enough to get my next hit, I wouldn't have ended up there. Are you sick and tired of prisons and jails?

After I got saved in prison, and while I was still locked up, I began to see that the people ridiculing Christians were the ones who were satisfied with their circumstances. They already figured they were coming back. They did nothing to change. Making fun of others gave them their excuse to reject God. Do you want to be a better man for your family? Do you realize your need for Jesus? Do you want to change?

TODAY'S GOAL:

Stop listening to people who do not have the courage to change. Follow hard after God.

Stephen Canup

FOR OUR FATHER'S GLORY

1 Corinthians 15:10 NKJV

But by the grace of God I am what I am, and His grace toward me was not in vain; but I labored more abundantly than they all, yet not I, but the grace of God which was with me.

My very best without God led me to defeat and prison. However, what the devil thought would destroy me, led me to God's grace, and into full-time ministry while still in prison. I studied, read God's Word, did Bible studies, went to chapel, listened to preachers on the radio, prayed, and fellowshipped with my God. I reached out to many on the prison compound. We would pray in the dorms, and on the yard. I shared God's love with everyone—always being respectful, that I might win some.

It's only by God's grace you have a second chance. Don't waste it. Share it with others. Be thankful. Learn to hear and obey God's voice. He will always be faithful to you. Keep your trust in Him and watch what He does.

And He said to me, "My grace is sufficient for you, for My strength is made perfect in weakness." Therefore most gladly I will rather boast in my infirmities, that the power of Christ may rest upon me (2 Corinthians 12:9).

TODAY'S GOAL:

Be led by Him, for His glory. When He speaks, obey, and give Him thanks for calling you out of misery, pain, and death.

Scott Heburn

THIRTY-DAY CHALLENGE

Joshua 1:8 NKJV

This Book of the Law shall not depart from your mouth, but you shall meditate in it day and night . . . For then you will make your way prosperous, and then you will have good success.

One day the Holy Spirit directed me to read the four Gospels (Matthew, Mark, Luke, and John), and the Book of Acts, three times in thirty days. This thirty-day challenge changed my life in a prison cell. The first time through these five books, He asked me to read it from an observer's perspective—listening to Jesus' words. The second time, from the disciple's perspective—hearing and doing the works. The third time, from Jesus' perspective—doing and speaking these Words. Each time through, I used a different colored pen or highlighter, to take notes of what Holy Spirit illuminated or taught me. By the third time through, an increased authority from Holy Spirit filled me with boldness and power. My prayer life changed. Revival broke out on the compound. Miracles, signs, and salvations began to occur like popcorn wherever He sent me. The yard, library, hallway, cell—it didn't matter where—because it was Jesus doing the same works again (Colossians 1:27).

TODAY'S GOAL:

Take the thirty-day challenge. Read Matthew, Mark, Luke, John, and Acts three times in thirty days. You will never be the same.

Jesus said, "*. . . whoever believes in me will do the works I have been doing, and they will do even greater things than these, because I am going to the Father*" (John 14:12).

David C. Hairabedian

TRUSTING

Proverbs 3:5-6 NKJV

Trust in the Lord with all your heart, And lean not on your own understanding; In all your ways acknowledge Him, And He shall direct your paths.

When we come from a lifestyle of not trusting anyone, it is hard to change. We don't trust men, don't trust women. Don't trust Mom and Dad.

How do we then trust someone we can't see? I'll tell you how. We start reading the Bible every day. We see how other people trusted the Lord in good times and bad. We start praying and fasting. We worship Him and keep reading the Word.

Many sorrows shall be to the wicked; But he who trusts in the Lord, mercy shall surround him (Psalm 32:10).

It's not easy being a Christian. Just try it and you will see. Trust the Lord each and every day.

He who dwells in the secret place of the most High, shall abide under the shadow of the Almighty . . . My God, in Him I will trust (Psalm 91:1-2).

TODAY'S GOAL:

So, begin today to give all your cares, all your desires, all your worries to the Lord.

He is faithful. He works all things out for your good. Be patient, we've spent years messing things up. Don't get mad at God if it doesn't get fixed overnight.

Ray Stribling

DAY AND NIGHT

Joshua 1:8 KJV

This book of the law shall not depart out of thy mouth; but thou shalt meditate therein day and night, that thou mayest observe to do according to all that is written therein: for then thou shalt make thy way prosperous, and then thou shalt have good success.

I love this verse and hopefully you will too after today. One of my best friends was raised Catholic and converted to Christianity at age forty. When he became a born-again Christian, he fell in love with the Word of God and read constantly. One day while at his parents reading, his mom said, "Chuck, you used to be such a good Catholic and now all you do is read that Bible."

Chuck replied, "Mom, it says in Joshua, you shall meditate day and night. I have to read it day and night."

I believe it is written as a commandment from God that we are to meditate day and night in the Word. It has a promise. Then He will make our way prosperous and we will have good success. Jesus Christ saved me, but His Word is what changed me.

Do you want to be changed? Read and meditate on the Word day and night.

TODAY'S GOAL:

Start by asking God to give you a hunger for His Word. It is the only book ever written that the author will stand there and explain it to you.

Bill Corum

FOCUS ON OTHERS

Philippians 2:3-4 NKJV

Let nothing be done through selfish ambition or conceit, but in lowliness of mind let each esteem others better than himself. Let each of you look out not only for his own interests, but also for the interests of others.

Sometimes if I'm not careful I will spend most of my time thinking of myself, my problems, my accomplishments, my family, my stuff . . . my, my, my. I forget how important it is to keep the focus off myself, and instead think of and pray for others around me.

It is the nature of man to be selfish and self-centered. Don't be too hard on yourself. From the beginning of time, sin has caused people to look inward and to focus on themselves. When we trust Jesus, our focus turns outward, and our vision starts to include others. Allow God to show you that there is a bigger, broader picture to consider, such as your friend who just got busted and lost everything, or your cellie who just got a Dear John letter. Maybe even the C.O. who is having problems at home.

God tends to take care of me when I am caring for and praying for others. I may not even notice at first, but when I look back, I see that He has taken care of situations and things affecting my life.

TODAY'S GOAL:

Look around you. Get your eyes off yourself. Is there someone around you that needs your help and prayers today?

Phil Fisher

EVEN ON THE YARD

Jude 1:3-4 NKJV

Beloved, while I was very diligent to write to you concerning our common salvation, I found it necessary to write to you exhorting you to contend earnestly for the faith which was once for all delivered to the saints. For certain men have crept in unnoticed, who long ago were marked out for this condemnation, ungodly men, who turn the grace of our God into lewdness and deny the only Lord God and our Lord Jesus Christ.

According to Jude, we must contend diligently in these days to keep the faith and not be swayed by certain doctrines that say—all that is needed to follow Jesus, is grace. Grace always goes with obedience. It's easy to follow God when we are in the chapel, but what about when we are out on the yard or in the gym? What happens when we run into the argument that God doesn't really require diligence? We must maintain our focus on Jesus.

We've all been out on the yard and the temptation to deny our faith is put in front of us. We should be ready in our hearts for this moment. The good news is, Jude also says God is able to keep us from stumbling (Jude 24).

TODAY'S GOAL:

Think about the cost of serving God each day. Pray for strength for obedience before you run into the ones that will mock you for your faith. Ask the Lord to keep you from stumbling today. *Lisa Stribling*

BUILD ON THE ROCK!

Matthew 7:24 NKJV

Therefore, whoever hears these sayings of mine and does them, I will liken him to a wise man who built his house on a rock: and the rain descended, the floods came, and the winds blew and beat on that house and it did not fall, for it was founded on the rock.

The Word of God must be everything to you. Anything that exists outside of it, though it may be truth, is a lie in comparison to the Word of God. Be jealous for your time with the Scriptures. Make a schedule for yourself and begin to search for the deep things of God in the pages He is giving us.

Build your house (your inner man) upon this. Don't mix mud and straw. Your entire house must be built of solid stone. Any weakness will not stand up against the winds that are sure to come. If your house is stone, but your roof is made of mud and straw, then a simple rain can take it out. The whole of you must be built soundly on the Word of God. Earthly wisdom abounds from everywhere, but the wisdom of God is only there for those who seek it. Don't become complacent, make your life's goal to build your inner man (your house) on the Word of God.

TODAY'S GOAL:

Sit down and write a schedule for the Word, and more time for prayer, and again more time for the Word. Live your life in thirty-minute increments.

Richy Bickle

MY CONFESSION OF FAITH

Mark 9:23 NKJV

"If you can believe, all things are possible to him who believes."

Father God, in the name of Jesus, I thank You that Your Word is true. I believe it all—100%.

You said You would never leave me or forsake me, so I thank You that You are right here with me. Lord God, because You are my Light and my Salvation, who shall I fear? How could I be afraid of anyone or anything?

Jesus, You are my Healer, my Peace, and my Joy. I look to You and rejoice that I am counted worthy to suffer for Your name's sake. I will glory in tribulations so that the power of God might be revealed in me.

Holy Spirit, You are my Helper, my Counselor, and You comfort me in all situations. You are in me and always with me.

Who or what can separate me from Your love, Father God? No tribulation, no distress, no peril, no sword. Nothing. No one.

I am more than a conqueror through Christ Jesus and because of Your love for me.

Father, Your grace is more than sufficient to overcome all situations.

Lord, You are good and Your mercy endures forever. Therefore, I am full of joy. My destiny is sure, and it is sealed forever. The joy of the Lord is my strength. I will dwell in the house of the Lord forever.

TODAY'S GOAL:

Repeat this prayer twice a day. Your love for God will increase.

Don Castleberry

FAITH BIGGER THAN FEAR

Hebrews 11:1 NKJV

Now faith is the substance of things hoped for,
the evidence of things not seen.

The real source of hope and help is in Christ Jesus. This holds true whether you are in a jail cell, prison, a drug rehab, or sitting in the Hills of Tennessee. I have been there, and I know the pain and personal heartache of waking up to a life full of hopelessness. It is only through the Lord Jesus Christ that we can find the hope and help we need.

A few years ago, I faced some major circumstances because of all the baggage of my past. I was applying for a promotion at work, and really praying and seeking the Lord. While shopping with my wife, I noticed a little wooden plaque, *Let Your Faith be Bigger Than Your Fear.* I bought it and put it in my living room. I took a picture of it with my cell phone and I look at it every day.

God worked in my heart to build up my faith to trust His promise in Hebrews 11:1. I began to realize that this is a walk of faith, not sight. Praise God, I got the job. A few years later, another promotion and more. I learned that walking by faith and not by sight, doesn't always mean you will get what you want, but even when things don't work out, faith is still all part of the plan. God has a purpose and a plan for our lives. Just learn to live and walk in it.

TODAY'S GOAL:

Ask God to give you faith that will override your fear (Psalm 56:3).

Mickey Park

GOD LOVES PRISONERS

Psalm 102:19-20 NIV

The Lord looked down . . . from Heaven . . .

to hear the groans of the prisoners . . .

God must have special love and attention reserved for people like us—prisoners, convicts, inmates, and captives. In fact, Strong's Concordance listed over 340 verses where the word *prison, prisoner, captive*, or *captivity* is a key word.

The Lord . . . does not despise His captive people . . . (Psalm 69:33).

I will free your prisoners from the waterless pit . . . You prisoners of hope; even now I announce that I will restore twice as much to you (Zechariah 9:11-12).

I was in prison and you came to visit me (Matthew 25:36).

Also, in one of His first talks in the synagogue, Jesus quoted Isaiah 61:1 . . . *the Lord has anointed me to preach good news to the poor. He has sent me to bind up the broken-hearted, to proclaim freedom for the captives and release from darkness for the prisoners . . .*

God has compassion for those in bondage. He listens, and He wants to set them free. Even though you are incarcerated, you can be free. I was in several prisons of my own making, long before I ever heard a succession of steel doors slam behind me. Going to prison set me free forever, after God found me and saved me right there on my prison bunk.

TODAY'S GOAL:

Tell the Father you want true freedom through Jesus by His Holy Spirit. Be free on the inside.

Stephen Canup

JESUS, GIVE ME STRENGTH

Philippians 4:11-13 NKJV

Not that I speak in regard to need, for I have learned in whatever state I am, to be content: I know how to be abased, and I know how to abound. Everywhere and in all things I have learned both to be full and to be hungry, both to abound and to suffer need. I can do all things through Christ who strengthens me.

When I was in prison, I kept a journal of the things I wanted to do when I got out. Twenty years later, I read through that journal again, and realized that with Christ strengthening me I had accomplished everything I wrote.

I have a wife, children, a home, an education, and a ministry reaching out to the over two million incarcerated in the United States. All because I put my faith and trust in Christ.

Thank the Holy Spirit for guiding you to make better decisions. *However, when He, the Spirit of Truth, has come, He will guide you into all truth; for He will not speak on His own authority, but whatever He hears He will speak; and He will tell you things to come* (John 16:13).

TODAY'S GOAL:

Keep your faith in Him, knowing He can do a lot better for you and your family than you have done. Trust in Christ's strength for your life. Remember your family is counting on you.

Scott Heburn

ABSTINENCE VS DELIVERANCE

John 8:36 NKJV

Therefore if the Son makes you free, you shall be free indeed . . .

The difference between abstinence and deliverance is the difference between night and day. Most Christians are abstaining, but not delivered. They're still religious, following rules but not experiencing the liberty that Christ paid to set us free. Abstinence is when you are abstaining, not actively sinning, but something inside you still wants to. Deliverance is when you've been set free, unchained from the bondage.

I was abstaining for thirteen years. I fought sin, fasted, prayed, read the Word, and abstained. But I wasn't delivered. Then one day, a visiting minister laid his hand on my head and suddenly said, "Iniquity, I break your power!" Like a rubber band, something broke out of me, and I was free. The cord of iniquity I was born with was broken (Psalms 51:5). I was delivered. The very desire to sin in that area was gone, vanished. Jesus will do the same for you.

TODAY'S GOAL:

Ask Jesus to transfer you from the religious world of abstinence to His liberating Kingdom of deliverance right now. He will do the same for you as He did for me (Acts 10:34).

Scripture-based proclamation for strength: *He has delivered us from the power of darkness and conveyed us into the kingdom of the Son of His love* (Colossians 1:13).

David Hairabedian

THE LIAR

John 8:44 NIV

You belong to your father, the devil, and you want to carry out your father's desires. He was a murderer from the beginning, not holding to the truth, for there is no truth in him. When he lies, he speaks his native language, for he is a liar and the father of lies.

I had a daddy problem! I did not realize this until my fifth time to prison. You see, I received a lie from the father of lies and I believed what that lie said about me until I became the lie. When we do not know the truth (Jesus) we can easily be deceived (John 14:6; Titus 3:3; Job 15:31; Galatians 6:7).

One day while in prison pursuing the truth (Jesus), our Bible study volunteer asked me if I wanted to have a talk with Jesus (the truth) and I said yes. This Christian volunteer led me to the truth (Jesus) and I had a vision of the first lie I received from the father of lies. I started crying right there in the prison group. I knew where I was deceived when I was nine-years old. I had been carrying that for over forty years. From that day on, I pursued nothing but the truth in the Word of God and with the people of God, and it started to transform my life (Romans 12:2). The Bible says that knowing the truth will set you free (John 8:32).

TODAY'S GOAL:

Ask God through the power of the Holy Spirit to show you where the lie came into your life. Then allow the Holy Spirit to lead you to all Truth.

Spencer Lindsay

SHOWING MERCY

Luke 10:30-33 NKJV

Then Jesus answered and said: "A certain man went down from Jerusalem to Jericho, and fell among thieves, who stripped him of his clothing, wounded him, and departed, leaving him half dead. Now by chance a certain priest came down that road. And when he saw him, he passed by on the other side. But a certain Samaritan, as he journeyed, came where he was. And when he saw him, he had compassion.

Every day we witness people getting caught up in bad situations like the man on the road to Jericho. When I was in prison, there wasn't a day go by, that I didn't see that happen. Maybe even people who have done us wrong and now we have the opportunity to make them pay or to show them kindness. Which one do you think God would want us to be and do? The answer is in the Word of God. Matthew 5:7 says if we want mercy, we have to show mercy.

TODAY'S GOAL:

When given the opportunity, are you the one who's still robbing people like the old days? Or even participating with others when they are choosing to do others wrong? Or are you one who is learning what it means to be like God and show mercy? *Ray Stribling*

DO AS I SAY

James 1:22-24 KJV

But be ye doers of the word, and not hearers only, deceiving your own selves. For if any be a hearer of the word, and not a doer, he is like unto a man beholding his natural face in a glass: For he beholdeth himself, and goeth his way, and straightway forgetteth what manner of man he was.

Does the title of the reading today sound like a correctional officer or a cop? It's not. It is God. Actually, the brother of Jesus wrote the book of James, but the Bible says all Scripture is inspired by God (II Timothy 3:16-17).

I spent almost forty years of my life trying to deceive people. I would cheat on my wives or girlfriends, but they had better not cheat on me. Why? Because I didn't want to be deceived. I would lie to someone, but I didn't want to be lied to. Why? Because I didn't want to be deceived.

Try and picture your own face. You can't. You have to look at a picture or look in the mirror (or stainless steel) to see what you look like. As soon as you walk away, you can't remember what you saw. Just like the verse above says. If you don't want to be deceived, do what the Bible says.

TODAY'S GOAL:

Read this passage until you understand that you are the one getting deceived if you don't do what God's Word says. *Bill Corum*

JUST HAVIN' A LITTLE TALK

Ephesians 6:18 NKJV

Praying always with all prayer and supplication in the Spirit, being watchful to this end with all perseverance and supplication for all the saints—

Some people don't like to talk very much. It's almost uncomfortable to be around them, because there are those quiet pauses where nothing is being said. Then there are those other folks who won't let you get a word in edgewise.

One thing I found out when I first got God in my life, was that I could talk to Him anytime and it didn't matter how much. As a matter of fact, it was the more the merrier when I talked to Him. I was in prison, and I would be walking around the yard on the track, reflecting on His creation. Then when I felt I really needed to have a serious talk with Him, I would go to my cell and get on my knees next to my bunk and bare my heart to Him. No one else knew what I had to say. It was just me and Him.

I still talk to God every day because it is the more the merrier when I talk to Him. He still listens and answers almost all my prayers. I try not to worry about the ones He doesn't answer or is quiet on because I know He intends the very best for me.

TODAY'S GOAL:

Have you taken time to talk with God lately? Give it a try. God is never too busy to hear from you.

Phil Fisher

I BLEW IT!

Jeremiah 1:5-10 NKJV

Before I formed you in the womb I knew you; Before you were born I sanctified you; I ordained you a prophet to the nations. Then said I: "Ah Lord I cannot speak for I am a youth." But the Lord said to me: "Do not say, I am a youth, For you shall go to all whom I send you . . ."

It does not matter what circumstance caused you to be stuck in some prison cell. God says the call on your life is still valid if you want it. He knew you before you were formed in the womb. Imagine that. He knew you would be where you are even before that fateful day in court put you there, and He still wants you. I see three things God was wanting from them in this passage in Jeremiah. And we get to use those same three things today to validate the call on our lives.

Stop voicing your disqualifications. Obediently speak what you know about Jesus when it's appropriate. And most of all, refuse to fear. He can't use you if you feel you blew it. He is with you even in your mistakes.

TODAY'S GOAL:

Learn today that you can accomplish the call on your life even while you are locked up. Ask God to ordain and send people your way, who want to hear about Him. Read the whole book of Jeremiah and ask God to show you when and where it applies to your life.

Lisa Stribling

I LIKE VIOLENCE

Matthew 11:12 NKJV

And from the days of John the Baptist until now the kingdom of heaven suffers violence, and the violent take it by force.

Now we're talking my language, but it's not the violence you think. It's violence of the Spirit, for we do not battle against flesh and blood, but spirits of the air. You have a unique opportunity to cause Satan some real problems right from your bunk.

Through prayer, we enter the most ancient of battles and all that we have to do is not quit. Your fellow cons will get saved, your children will stop getting high, your relationships will be healed, and the enemy begins to fear your name.

You want the greatest fight of your life? Then grab your sword and jump into the fray! Be dangerous for the first time in your life. You have suffered too much at the hands of the enemy. Now it's time to take the battle to him. You are surrounded by the enemy's generals. Begin to turn them into God's generals. Shatter the trophy case of the devil and take his most prized possessions. In the name of the Lord, raid the heart of the enemy camp.

TODAY'S GOAL:

Walk the yard with your fellow Christian brothers or sisters and begin to claim the blood of Jesus over every square inch of the compound. You have the power of the Holy Spirit inside of you. Nothing is impossible through God. You just need to have the faith for it.

Richy Bickle

FOLLOW ME

Matthew 16:24 KJV

Then said Jesus unto his disciples, If any man will come after me, let him deny himself, and take up his cross, and follow me.

Jesus calls us to follow Him. He shares this calling over and over throughout the Scriptures. His message to the heart is—*If any man will come after me, let him deny himself, and take up his cross, and follow me.* The call is to follow Him, not your home boys, road dogs, or besties. Not this gang, or that gang, or this affiliation, or that affiliation, but follow Jesus. It is not when you walk out of jail or prison, or when you get into better circumstances, more money, or a better job. It says to *follow me* where you are right now, right here. The greatest decision I ever made in my life was to follow Jesus. Please consider that today.

TODAY'S GOAL:

I am challenging you today. Give Him a chance. You have tried everything else. How's that working out for you? I'm guessing not so good. Try Jesus. Follow Him. *If any man will come after me, let him deny himself, and take up his cross, and follow me.*

Mickey Park

CAN GOD USE YOU?

2 Samuel 12:9 NKJV

(God said to David) Why have you despised the commandment of the LORD, *to do evil in His sight? You have killed Uriah the Hittite with the sword; you have taken his wife to be your wife . . .*

Throughout the Bible, we find God using some of the most unlikely people to accomplish His will to advance His Kingdom. He's used murderers, adulterers, thieves, lowly shepherds, hated tax collectors—and a lot of them, at one time or another, had been in some form of confinement or captivity.

But these men repented, committed their lives to God, and cried out to Him from their own miserable circumstances. People like Peter, Paul, Samson, James, John the Baptist, Joseph, and Jeremiah had been incarcerated just like us. Leaders like Moses, David, and Jacob—who were once murderers, adulterers, and thieves—were used mightily once they called on God and turned their lives back to Him. Even Jesus was arrested and put on trial.

God does not care about your record. Unlike men, He does not discriminate against the down-trodden, the lowly, the forgotten—we who are labeled as felons, prisoners, convicts, and inmates. Yes, God can use even me and you.

TODAY'S GOAL:

Confess your sins to God. He already knows all of them anyway. As you truly humble yourself before Him, thank Him for His forgiveness found in Jesus Christ alone. Be real. Have an honest talk with Him. Ask God to use you in His Kingdom.

Stephen Canup

GOD IS FAITHFUL

Proverbs 3:5-6 NKJV

Trust in the Lord with all your heart, And lean not on your own understanding; In all your ways acknowledge Him, And He shall direct your paths.

Jesus is always faithful, giving good things to His children. Proverbs 3:5-6 was among the first Scriptures I learned in prison. It took a long time for these truths to get from my head to my heart.

Today, I trust Him with every aspect of my life—my wife, children, ministry, and finances. He is able. Every Scripture I read in the Bible has come true like I never could have imagined. Even while in prison, growing in this faith, God kept me in His love and grace.

I encourage you to invite God's love and purpose to become your life. Our God is always faithful and wants the best for us and our families. Today, dig into the Word of God, memorize these Scriptures, cry out to Him for help. He is always with us. Do not trust in your old angry, lustful, deceptive, manipulative ways. We've been shucking and jiving for too long. Who cares what those around you think? Get out of the driver's seat, jump in the back seat, and enjoy your new ride.

TODAY'S GOAL:

Be all in for Jesus. Keep your great ideas out of it and watch the peace, love, and life He will bring to you and your loved ones. Thank Him for loving you so much and allowing you a second chance to do it His way.

Scott Heburn

STAY ON TRACK

James 1:25 NKJV

But he who looks into the perfect law of liberty and continues in it, and is not a forgetful hearer but a doer of the work, this one will be blessed in what he does.

This is one of my favorite Scriptures because when the Holy Spirit downloaded this into me and I received it, it became foundational. I founded Working Men of Christ Ministry on this same Scripture. I always had a desire for the Word but would become distracted and didn't follow through. In this Scripture today, it says *and continues in it*. When I continued in the Word no matter what happened to me or where I found myself, I started to not forget what I read. And as I learned to hear more by continuing, the Holy Spirit gave me work to do (my assignment).

This Scripture played out in my life behind prison bars. Once you stay in the Word long enough to hear what the Spirit has to say to you, you will be blessed. No matter where you find yourself (John 14:25-26; 1 Corinthians 2:6-15).

Stay on track with the Word of God. It is able to save your soul (James 1:21).

TODAY'S GOAL:

Ask the Holy Spirit to help you continue in God's Word. Then start listening for your assignment.

Spencer Lindsay

DEFERRED HOPE

Proverbs 13:12 NIV

Hope deferred makes the heart sick, but a longing fulfilled is a tree of life.

Deferred hope almost killed me fifteen years into my sentence. It crept in slow and quiet like a serpent wraps around your body and squeezes the life force out. Its negative thoughts began to subtly enter my heart. King Solomon warned, *Above all else, guard your heart, for it is the wellspring of life* (Proverbs 4:23 *paraphrased*). Once a heart is polluted, bad decisions follow.

When God's promises are delayed, hope deferred shows up in three distinct ways: (1) very real circumstances like you're still in prison, sick, and etcetera; (2) well-intentioned words of family and friends like, "Well, maybe God put you here to help someone else" or "this is for your own good"; (3) a serpent begins speaking in your ear, "Where is the promise of his coming? He delivered others but forgot about you." Once this triple-braided cord of deferred hope wraps around your life, recognize the enemy and call on Jesus, the Hope Restorer.

TODAY'S GOAL:

Jesus will break Satan's ropes and chains from your life in an instant. Call out to Him now. Scripture-based proclamation for strength: *For ye have need of patience, that, after ye have done the will of God, ye might receive the promise* (Hebrews 10:36). *Knowing this, that the trying of your faith worketh patience* (James 1:3). *If any of you lacks wisdom, let him ask of God, who gives to all liberally and without reproach, and it will be given to him* (James 1:5).

David Hairabedian

WORKING TOO HARD

Ephesians 2:8-9 NKJV

For by grace you have been saved through faith, and that not of yourselves; it is the gift of God, not of works, lest anyone should boast.

Recently, I was bombarded with thoughts of what I was personally doing for God as far as ministry was concerned. When I first received Christ into my heart in prison, I was so happy. I wanted to spread the gospel and do whatever I could to get others on the same track I was.

While this is an admirable endeavor, and a command of God, we should keep this in perspective and try not to get caught up in a salvation-by-works mentality. God still loves me even if I never preached another sermon, but He also needs me. So, if you find that you feel you are or aren't doing enough for God, just talk to Him. He will put your mind at ease. Then look around, and you will see all kinds of opportunities to serve Him. Just don't get caught up in thinking that what you do makes Him love you more or love you less.

It's what He has already done that proves His love for us. And that, my friend, is what He did when He shed His precious blood for us on the cross of Calvary.

TODAY'S GOAL:

Do you feel burned out by all the good works that you are doing for God? Take time today to rest in the salvation He has provided. Even Jesus had to get away and pray.

Phil Fisher

KNOWING GOD'S WILL FOR YOUR LIFE

Ephesians 5:17 NKJV

Therefore, do not be unwise, but understand what the will of the Lord is.

Until you know God's will for your life, you can really make a mess of things. I sure did. Sitting in a prison cell, I finally discovered God's will. Everything changed! It can change for you too. Once you know God's will, your purpose becomes clear. You become a man or woman on a mission. Heaven's power backs you. Supernatural peace, joy, and purpose encompass you. You become a changed person.

Do you want to know His will? This may surprise you, but God's will begins at the same spot for everyone—the filling station. *Be filled with the Holy Spirit* (Ephesian 5:18). The disciples didn't begin their ministry until they were filled with the Holy Spirit (see Acts 2:1-41). Prior to being filled with the Holy Spirit they were hiding in an upper room, confused, powerless, weak, and scared. Peter had just cut off a soldier's ear and then denied Christ three times. The moment they were filled with the Spirit, Peter became bold and fearless, leading 3,000 to Christ (Acts 2:41). These same men then "turned the world upside down" (Acts 17:6). Are you ready?

TODAY'S GOAL:

Pray, "Father, fill me with your Holy Spirit, and reveal my purpose today. I receive this by faith now, in Jesus' Name. Amen!

Scripture-based proclamation: *Don't be drunk with wine, because that will ruin your life. Instead, be filled with the Holy Spirit* (Ephesians 5:18).

David Hairabedian

Meet the 12

PHIL FISHER

Phil had just reached his teen years in the Missouri Ozark area when he started running down a road that had no end. Smoking a little grass and drinking a little beer couldn't be all that bad, he thought. He had no way of knowing it would lead to a needle addiction that lasted over two decades (shooting anything he could get into that needle). At age fifteen, he started going to juvenile and by age seventeen, had caught his first robbery case. He fled to California, but Missouri extradited him back, where he was facing thirty years. But he beat that time in prison and didn't even take into account that it might be due to his praying mama.

He headed back to California to take care of unfinished business. Sex, drugs, and rock and roll was his mission. Party and party some more, as long as there was a needle involved. Phil couldn't see that he was slipping deeper and deeper into a pit he'd never escape from. Over the next sixteen years, Phil ended up catching three separate felonies in California, the last being an assault on a police officer. He did sixteen years on the installment plan—in Folsom, Tracy, and seven other prisons.

His last trip to prison was a parole violation. While in reception, he was locked up in a tiny cell twenty-three hours a day. To keep from going stir crazy, he picked up the little New Testament he found and began to read. When the chaplain went cell to cell asking who wanted to go to chapel, Phil saw his opportunity to get out of his cell. Somewhere in all that, it happened. He went from being filthy Phil to just Phil. *If any man be in Christ, he is a new creature* (2 Corinthians 5:17).

He was released from prison on July 3, 1994. And he's never been back. Phil wasn't sure what going back to Missouri would be like. He loved his mom so much, but he had always hated his stepfather. But things seemed different this time. Phil had the love of Christ in his heart and was determined to go back and love him. He ended up leading his stepfather to Christ not long before he died. Phil was holding him in his arms when he went to heaven.

Phil was the worship leader in his church for over twenty years. Today, he owns his own business. God has blessed him with a wife, and they are very active in prison ministry.

Phil Fisher

PO Box 281

Lone Jack, MO 64070

2fishersministry@gmail.com

RICHY BICKLE

Richy's mother was a fifteen-year-old junkie. As a newborn, he and his mom lived in a car for that first year. For the next eleven-plus years of his life, he grew up in a drug house—a house where he was exposed to big-screen pornography, where cops kicked in the doors and dragged either his mom, or dad, or both off to jail. As a small child it wasn't uncommon for him to walk into the bathroom in the morning and find some stranger shooting dope. It was a house where beatings, stabbings, and shootings took place—even a murder before Richy was a teenager.

When he was twelve years old, his mom and dad got saved and their lives were radically changed. Richy, however, did not want to change. He wanted only one thing—to be a bigger, 'badder' drug dealer and gangster than they had been. He was sent to juvenile homes several times and escaped from every one of them. When he was sixteen, he caught an armed-robbery case and was sent to the oldest prison west of the Mississippi. Time Magazine dubbed the Missouri State Penitentiary the bloodiest forty-seven acres in America. Imagine going to a place like that as a sixteen-year-old boy. Richy survived that horrific experience and upon his release from prison continued in his life of crime and drugs for the next several years.

In 2004, he surrendered his life to the Lord Jesus Christ. God has blessed Richy with a godly wife and he is the father of four children. God uses him in powerful ways in the streets and prisons. Richy has a powerful anointing and is an amazing Bible teacher. He is an ordained minister and one of the leaders and teachers at the Hope City KC house of prayer and community center. Hope City seeks to bring social justice to the inner city of Kansas City through 24/7 prayer and missions.

Richy Bickle

Hope City KC
5101 E 24th St
Kansas City, MO 64127

DON CASTLEBERRY

Don was raised to work hard on a farm. He learned his work ethic through hard labor.

He found high school extremely boring, so at age seventeen he joined the U.S. Army and stayed for six years. In the army, he began drinking and partying hard.

When he was discharged, he became a bank-loan officer. While working there, he figured out how to embezzle money without getting caught. He got away with it for ten years, stealing lots of money and living high. During that time, he owned a couple of airplanes and flew around, partying.

One of the friends he partied with just so happened to be an FBI agent. In 1975, Don's conscience finally got the best of him and he turned himself in. It took the feds sixteen months to put together a solid case. He was facing over forty-two years, but by the grace of God they dismissed nineteen of the twenty-one counts and he was sentenced to six years.

Four months into his sentence, Don surrendered his life to Jesus by praying the "want to" prayer given to him by a Gideon volunteer. Don meant business on January 9, 1977 when he prayed that sinner's prayer. He knew within seconds that he was born again. Right after that, God did a miracle and he was released within a month of praying that prayer. The rest of his time he did on federal probation.

Don and the Gideon volunteer who lead him to Christ stayed friends until his friend went home to heaven in 2019. Don was privileged to officiate that Gideon's homecoming celebration.

God gave Don a heart for prisoners right from the start. His heart was changed forever. He longs to see prisoners born again and to have a life that has purpose.

Don Castleberry is the Founder/President of Freedom in Jesus Prison Ministries.

Don Castleberry
PO Box 939
Levelland, TX 79336
info@fijm.org

Don and his wife Donna co-founded Freedom in Jesus Ministries in 1985. Donna went home to heaven on March 2, 2020.

BILL CORUM

Bill rode over 2,500 miles in handcuffs, leg-irons, and waist-chains in his first twenty-one years of life. After his release from federal prison, he returned to his hometown of Kansas City, Missouri. He was determined to keep the goals he had set for himself—never go back to prison and never get caught. Bill's insatiable hunger for money, power, and influence drove him.

He spent the next eighteen years evading the law. Like a frog in a slow-boiling pot, he found himself in the ever-tightening vise-grip of drugs, pornography, prostitution, and organized crime. He was implicated as one of the leading cocaine dealers in Kansas City. He watched from the shadows as many of the other dealers he knew in the city were getting busted and killed. It was only a matter of time before he would be next. Finally, he found himself in so deep it looked as though there was no way out. After being arrested, he faced the probability of spending the rest of his life behind the walls.

In 1983, Bill said these words, "God, if You are real, and You can change me, I will live for You." His life was radically changed, and he couldn't deny the existence of God. Bill kept his end of the deal and gave complete control of his life to Jesus Christ. The first nine years he was a Christian, he read the Bible five hours a day.

God has given Bill a mandate to reach men and women who are locked up. He has been in prison ministry since 1988 and has visited over 500 prisons and jails across the United States and abroad.

Many times when Bill is speaking in a prison, he will hold up his Bible and say, "Jesus saved me, but His Word is what changed me." He not only got into the Word, but he let the Word get into him. His conversion and over-three decades of prison ministry are all told in his autobiography *The Ultimate Pardon.*

In Bill's book, he describes the ultimate pardon as God forgiving him, because he never received the pardon he fought so many years to get. But then, NEWS FLASH: On January 6, 2017—after twenty-two years and five governors—Bill Corum was granted a full pardon. His motto is, *never give up.*

Bill Corum
PO Box 281
Lone Jack, MO 64070
ppm@theultimatepardon.com

LISA STRIBLING

Lisa began sticking needles in her arm at the age of twelve. By age sixteen, she was a hardened junkie. After bouts of homelessness, she moved in with her boyfriend Ray and started down a long, hard road of crime and fifteen years of addiction to the needle. A few years later, they were married and started a family, even though they were not prepared to be parents. Their children were born into a drug house where they were exposed to fights, stabbings, shootings, and every other thing that goes with that lifestyle. Their children were passed from family member to family member every time the cops kicked in their door and drug them off to jail (this was before the state took away kids from unfit parents). As soon as they got out on bond, they'd go right back to the violence and abuse.

Lisa finally hit rock bottom. She caught a forgery case. When the smoke cleared, she found herself in a Missouri Penitentiary for women.

Hope found her in that state prison. She had nowhere to turn but to God. Lisa's story is one of transformation midst the most trying set of circumstances. When she and her husband Ray got saved, they left the streets. But they left their hearts behind.

So, they returned to the streets and co-founded and are the directors of Hope City KC, an inner-city ministry in one of the roughest neighborhoods in Kansas City, Missouri. Ray and Lisa have been together for over forty years. They have five children—some of whom are in ministry with them—and are grandparents to fourteen grandchildren. They give God all the glory for restoring their lives.

Hope City is a house of prayer and community center that seeks to bring social justice to the inner city of Kansas City through 24/7 prayer and missions. From the place of prayer, their community center feeds the hungry, the Trade-Off-Program (T.O.P.) helps the addicts, their youth program works with at-risk kids, and internships equip men and women to minister in the inner city.

Lisa Stribling
Hope City KC
5101 E 24th St
Kansas City MO 64127

RAY STRIBLING

Ray started down a dark road when he was only nine years old. There was no way he could have known at that age that huffing glue and paint was only the beginning, and that drinking at age ten would launch him into a full-blown addiction. Just a few short years later, Ray was an intravenous drug user, addicted like so many, to the needle itself.

At age eighteen, he met a cute but feisty sixteen-year old. They moved in together and started what became years of criminal activity. Their house was where the action was. Sex, drugs, and rock and roll. The other element that goes along with all that is violence. It lasted for years. Fights, shootings, stabbings, even a murder in their house.

About the time Ray and Lisa were married, he got stabbed (not by her, though they were at each other's throats). A guy stabbed him twice just missing his lung. Two years later in 1984, a man gut shot Ray at point-blank range. He was in the hospital for a month. It was a miracle that he lived. Some people might have slowed down or backed off from a lifestyle that gets you shot, stabbed, or dead—but not Ray Stribling. He went back out and ran harder than ever.

In January of 1990 in Kansas City's jail, MCI, there was an old man in the bunk next to Ray. The guy wouldn't shut up. Rays says he had a raspy voice and just kept saying over and over, "Yep that dope is from the devil. Yep, its gonna take all your money, its gonna take your kids. Yep that dope is from the devil. Devil the dope man. Yep, yep, gonna take it all."

Ray went to the Sunday night church service that week and when the preacher asked, "Is there anybody here sick and tired of the way your living?" Ray raised his hand and went forward and asked Jesus to take over his life and change him. He says that he had a rush better than any shot of dope he had ever done. Ray Stribling has never had a needle in his arm since that day.

Six months later, he went to trial and was sentenced to five years. He went to prison as a Christian and attended every Christian service offered by the prison. He had to say "no" many times when other inmates offered him drugs or whatever, but he always said no. That first "no" was hard, but Ray says they got easier. He stayed strong and came home serving Jesus. Ray and Lisa have been together for over forty years. In 2004, they founded Hope City KC, an inner-city ministry. Ray has led countless people to Jesus since his conversion. Ray and Lisa have five children and fourteen grandchildren.

Ray Stribling
Hope City KC
5101 E 24th St
Kansas City MO 64127

SPENCER LINDSAY

Spencer's world radically changed at age nine when his mother was taken from him because of cancer. But no one told him anything about why she was no longer with him. When the funeral came, and Spencer saw her in the casket, that's when the tears started falling and his life started to change. He went from being an innocent young man, to a deceived young man. Shortly after the funeral, the enemy (the devil) came and told him that his daddy was rich. And Spencer believed it. That lie began to lead his life from that moment on. He started acting out. His friends became his mother and father. Spencer turned on his dad and started stealing from him because he quit giving him money to finance his foolishness. Spencer says, 'Once you can steal from your own father, your neighbor becomes nothing'.

He started getting in trouble with small things and that grew to larger things. He wanted family so badly, he became a lieutenant in a clique. His duty was to infiltrate other cliques, peoples, and persons—robbing, stealing, manipulating, using dope, lying—achieving it for his new family by any means necessary. He started selling cocaine, but in doing so, he became a serious crack addict. This was the beginning of Spencer becoming a repeat offender—being locked up in all but one of the prisons in the state of Kansas.

But there was a calling on Spencer's life. In 1992, he had a born-again experience when he accepted Jesus Christ in jail. It was the beginning of change for him, but he still had the same mind set, soul wounds, and broken feelings. He wondered why his life didn't change. Seventeen years later, on his fifth time back to prison, the Holy Spirit enlightened him to the passage in Romans 12:2 . . . *but be transformed by the renewing of your mind.*

He made a conscious decision to renew his mind through the Word of God. When a volunteer came into the prison to do a Bible study, he asked Spencer if he wanted to have a personal talk with Jesus. Spencer said, "Yes!". While having his talk with Jesus, Spencer had a vision. He realized he had been traumatized at age nine when cancer snatched his mother from him.

After a year of renewing his mind, the Holy Spirit put *The Captivity Series* by Katie Souza in his path. By the third chapter, he was caught up in the material of her book. By the last chapter he knew his own purpose and his expected end. He had a plan from God to start a Bible correspondence incentive course using *The Captivity Series Workbook*. Before he was released from prison, he had the entire vision written out for the course.

God then vacated his sentence and released him into a discipleship home where Spencer became the leader of that home and ministry before starting his own ministry. Today, Working Men of Christ (WMOC) has over 1800 inmates enrolled in Spencer's correspondence courses. They have eight discipleship homes. He is a chaplain at Shawnee County Detention Center and is a mentor for Kansas Department of Corrections. As an ordained minister he wears many hats.

Spencer Lindsay
PO Box 47491
Wichita, KS 67201
wmocinfo@gmail.com

KATIE SOUZA

Katie Souza didn't always walk in the presence and power of God. In fact, for many years she lived a violent and drug-addicted life. Katie started experimenting with drugs as a teenager. When her media career took off, her drug use escalated. She worked as a model and actress, but drugs caused her to lose job after job, so she turned further to crime to support herself.

Katie's life consisted of drugs, clandestine laboratories, stolen vehicles, high-speed chases, gun shoot-outs, and a dozen arrests in one year. When she was finally captured by federal marshals in February of 1999, she was at the end of her rope. Charged with manufacturing, conspiracy, and gun possession, Katie was sentenced to twelve-and-a-half years in a federal prison.

The pressures of her circumstances finally drove her into the arms of God. As Katie began her long incarceration, the Holy Spirit gave her a hunger for the Word. Soon after, she started a Bible study within her cellblock. One-night, God told Katie she would have a new release date. Eighteen months later, His word came to pass, and miraculously seven years were taken off her sentence. Her out date was the exact month and day God spoke to her (this is well-documented because she had announced the details to everyone she knew for months in advance).

While still in prison, Katie began writing her first book, *The Captivity Series: The Key to Your Expected End*, which is now in huge demand by inmates around the world (300,000 books have been given to inmates).

In 2004, she married Robert Souza who served seventeen years in prison. Within two years, the Lord blessed them with a new home, a successful business, and a promising prison ministry.

Katie Souza's entries in this book are excerpts from her books: *Healing the Wounded Soul* and *The Captivity Series.*

Katie Souza Ministries
PO Box 1289
Maricopa, AZ 85139

MICKEY PARK

From an early age, Mickey had to learn to fight. At school, other kids ridiculed him for his hillbilly accent. At home, his parents were raging alcoholics. By the age of ten, he already hated his life. He was angry. He began picking fights just for kicks. Then came the alcohol. Drugs soon followed. By his teens he was a hopeless addict, living for the next high and willing to do just about anything to get it. Mickey drank, toked, and fought his way across America, Canada, and Europe, looking for the next opportunity to get stoned. He always found it and when he did, he found out there were always consequences to pay.

Mickey's life on the streets naturally led to a life of crime. He graduated quickly from petty theft to strong-armed robbery just to feed his habit. And then, the big time—a murder charge. After agreeing to a plea deal for first-degree murder, Mickey received a sentence of ninety-nine years.

He contemplated suicide. In his despair, he remembered the one Christian he had known in his life—his grandmother. In his jail cell, he fell to his knees and began to pray. At the age of twenty-five, with nowhere to run and no hope for the future, he gave his life over to Jesus.

The former 'hillbilly alcoholic drug addict', as he liked to call himself, was now a child of the living God. For the first time in his life, Mickey felt alive. He began to share his testimony with other inmates. Eventually, Mickey earned his master's degree in ministry from Luther Rice Seminary and met a young missionary girl who would become his wife—all while still behind bars.

Today, Mickey is a free man with a real family. Granted parole by God's amazing grace, he lives with his wife and daughter in a home that overlooks the beautiful hills of Tennessee, where he was born. But he still spends a lot of time behind bars, visiting inmates and sharing his story in hopes of reaching one more lost life for Christ.

Mickey Park
PO Box 253
New Hope, TN 37380
setfree@setfreetoserveministry.org

STEPHEN CANUP

Stephen never dreamed he would be starting a prison sentence at age fifty-six. It should not have surprised him though since he had been running from God for twenty years. In fact, he hadn't truly served Him for forty years.

Twenty years earlier, Stephen was living the *American Dream*. In 1987, he was a partner in the world's largest accounting firm and earning well into six-figures. He had a beautiful wife and a healthy son. He was building a new home, and his credit was spotless. But Stephen wasn't satisfied with who he was and what he had accomplished. He wanted more. In 1989, he left his wife and son to pursue fame and riches in Nashville's music business.

But trying to break into the music business was nearly impossible. He felt incredibly stupid. For the first time in his life, he had failed—and failed miserably. He had lost everything. In his pain, he turned to alcohol, marijuana, crack cocaine, gambling, sex, and pornography. For several years he was in deep depression and often contemplated suicide.

Finally, in May of 2008, he was arrested in a shelter for violating the terms of his probation from a previous crime. He was sent to CCA, Nashville's medium-security federal prison, to serve his time. He thought his life was over.

Almost a year into his prison sentence, he finally cried out in true humility and brokenness and surrendered to God. God heard Stephen's cry and lifted him out of the pit of hopelessness and despair. On April 20, 2009, Stephen re-dedicated his life to Christ and was re-baptized. He says that even though he was still locked up, he was *free on the inside*.

Today, Stephen is still in prison, but he gets to go home at the end of each day. He has dedicated the rest of his life to reaching out to the incarcerated and to sharing the love of Jesus Christ.

Stephen is the executive director and vice president of *Freedom in Jesus Prison Ministry*, which helps inmates in many ways. His ministry evangelizes and baptizes through weekend crusades and revivals in prisons and helps men and women upon release.

Stephen Canup
PO Box 939
Levelland, TX 79336
info@fijm.org

Scott Heburn

Scott grew up in Tallahassee and was 'the wrong crowd' his mom always warned him to stay away from. By age ten, he was a full-blown vandal, breaking windows out of cars and trailers on sales lots. He started drinking at twelve-years old. When he became violent against other kids, his mom took him to counseling. Before each session he took Quaaludes, and within minutes the therapists would be done with him. They labeled him Psychopathic.

Later in life, they called his condition Antisocial Personality Disorder. He thought that was better. But it turned out that it was the new name for Psychopathic. He was skipping school, partying with girls, stealing everything he could at ages thirteen and fourteen. On foot or on motorcycle, it didn't matter, he ran from the cops until it all stopped when he hit a dump truck on a bike going 80 mph. Scott was pronounced dead at the hospital, but he lived. During his month's stay, he cussed the nurses out and smoked in his room. He left there in a full body cast and started partying again, hitting people with crutches, falling down, hiding dope in his cast.

At fifteen, he entered a drug program and worked the AA steps. He stayed sober until age seventeen. After going through the ninth grade three times, he settled for a GED. Within a week of turning eighteen, he was back to partying, fighting in bars, fighting police, dealing drugs, and robbing people. He was out of control, arrested twenty times by age twenty.

Scott went through drug treatment, halfway houses, jails, and was off to prison for the first time. When released, he received a $25,000 settlement from his motorcycle wreck and began partying and running from the cops again.

By age twenty-four, he had been arrested over thirty times. He jumped bond for burglary in Florida, was a fugitive from justice in Georgia, was picked up by a SWAT team for armed robbery and faced life in prison. He cussed out the judge and told him, 'I did my crimes now give me my time'.

A guy in jail told him about Jesus. Scott didn't know what he was talking about. When he got to prison, his crack dealer from the streets invited him to church. He picked up a tract that said if he confessed his sins, he could have a new life. That sounded good. For three nights, he confessed his sins and asked God to please give him a new life.

Thank God, He did! Scott took eight Bible studies, went to three Bible colleges, attended chapel, read the Bible, and prayed. Five years later when he was released from prison, he got his bachelor's degree, got married, bought a home, and had two children. The full story of God's redemption is in Scott's book, *Chaos and Prison, Now New Life*. Scott spends every day trying to reach as many of the 2.5 million men and women incarcerated in the United States as he possibly can.

Scott Heburn
PO Box 1453
Live Oak Florida 32064

DAVID HAIRABEDIAN

David was a naturally gifted athlete. He was the co-captain of the wrestling team in high school, district champion, regional champ, and a martial-arts champion. He came from a good family and was enrolled in college. At age nineteen, he was making his own way, working part time (twenty hours a week) as a clerk in a grocery store for $3.50 an hour. It doesn't seem like much money ($70.00 a week), but at the time it was fair.

David didn't do or sell drugs, but he knew a guy who bought drugs, and another who sold them. So, he brokered a deal. While on his break in the grocery store parking lot, he made more money in two minutes than he made working in the store an entire week. David said, "After that, it was on like Donkey Kong." He went from selling grams, to quarter ounces, to ounces. Business kept growing until finally he was trading stolen jets for cocaine.

He owned watch stores, sunglass stores, and other businesses, trying his best to get out of the drug business. By age twenty-four, he was worth a million dollars on Dunn and Bradstreet. But his plan to go legit was too late.

The sun was shining as the Cessna Citation taxied toward David and his team waiting on the tarmac of an executive airfield in Florida. The pilot had agreed, for a price, to deliver the plane to be used for cocaine trafficking by the Cali Cartel. David clutched the satchel of cash they'd agreed upon. This was the second plane they'd stolen in a month. Within seconds, unmarked cars sped toward them and twenty heavily armed federal agents surrounded them.

This would not be an orange juice morning in South Florida. In fact, it would be a long time before David was free again. He spent one thousand hamburger days (twenty years) in federal prison—entering the system at twenty-five and coming out at forty-five.

For David, pulling chain was the beginning of his journey to freedom. While languishing in a roach-infested cell in Leavenworth Penitentiary his mother was praying. Jesus responded to those prayers by appearing to David in his prison cell, and his life was forever changed (read his whole story in *Jet Ride to Hell, Journey to Freedom*).

Thirty years later, he is the founder of Virtual Church Media which reaches 120 million homes on five continents, and Heart of America Prison Ministries providing Bibles to prisoners in more than 1,000 facilities. He is the author of thirty discipleship booklets. He and his beautiful wife Joanna host a television broadcast to help others discover their God-given gifts and callings. They live in California.

David Hairabedian
www.virtualchurchmedia.com
1835 Newport Blvd
Building A109 #333
Costa Mesa CA 92627